MUSIC COMPOSITION

submit@uremusic.com

Printed in the United States of America

First Printing, 2011

Printed Date: 2019 (revised 5/20)

www.uremusic.com

www.kevinure.com

www.themusicalcore.com

Table of Contents

CHAPTER 1: THE GENESIS 8

A FUGUE A DAY 12
USING THIS BOOK 16

CHAPTER 2: DAILY ROUTINE 19

MOTIVATION 21
INSPIRATION 27
INSPIRATION CORRALLING TOOLS 28

CHAPTER 3: THE COMPOSING HOUR 31

THE COMPOSING HOUR SCHEDULE 33
ROUTINE TRIGGERS 36

PART I: TECHNIQUE 39

SUMMARY OF EXERCISES 39
COMPOSING EFFECTIVELY 40
COMPOSITION EXERCISES 40
DAILY ROUTINE PROGRAM (WORKBOOK) 42

CHAPTER 4: THE RHYTHMIC MOTOR 43

EXERCISE 1.1 (MM=60) 47
BEGINNING STAGE 48
BEGINNING EXERCISE 50
INTERMEDIATE STAGE 51
INTERMEDIATE EXERCISE 54
ADVANCED STAGE 55
ADVANCED EXERCISE 57

Exercise Tips **59**
Summary **61**
Ear Training No. 1 .... **63**
Daily Routine No. 1 64
Mirror Exercise No. 1 67

Chapter 5: The Overtone Drone **68**

Beginning Stage **73**
Beginning Exercise 74
Intermediate Stage **76**
Intermediate Exercise 77
Advanced Stage **78**
Advanced Exercise 78
Exercise Tips **79**
Summary **81**
Ear Training No. 2 .... **82**
Daily Routine No. 2 83
Mirror Exercise No. 2 86

Chapter 6: The Melodic Line **87**

Beginning Stage **90**
Beginning Exercise 90
Intermediate Stage **91**
Intermediate Exercise 91
Advanced Stage **92**
Advanced Exercise 92
Exercise Tips **93**
Summary **93**
Ear Training No. 3 .... **94**
Daily Routine No. 3 95
Mirror Exercise No. 3 98
Mirror Exercise No. 4 99

Chapter 7: Harmonic Backdrops **100**

Completing the Exercises **101**
Beginning Stage **102**
Beginning Exercise 103
Intermediate Stage **105**
Intermediate Exercise 106
Advanced Stage **107**
Exercise Tips **110**
Summary **110**
Ear Training No. 4 .... **111**
Daily Routine No. 4 112
Mirror Exercise No. 5 115
Mirror Exercise No. 6 116

PART II: COUNTERPOINT **117**

CHAPTER 8: FIRST SPECIES COUNTERPOINT **119**

First Species Exercise **120**
Ear Training No. 5 .... **123**
Daily Routine No. 5 124
Mirror Exercise No. 7 128
Mirror Exercise No. 8 129

CHAPTER 9: SECOND SPECIES COUNTERPOINT **130**

Second Species Exercise **131**
Ear Training No. 6 .... **134**
Daily Routine No. 6 135
Mirror Exercise No. 9 139
Mirror Exercise No. 10 140

CHAPTER 10: THIRD SPECIES COUNTERPOINT **141**

Third Species Exercise **142**
Ear Training No. 7 .... **144**
Daily Routine No. 7 145

Mirror Exercise No. 11 150
Mirror Exercise No. 12 151
Additional Ear Training Exercises 152

Part III: Composing Music Guide 153

Chapter 11: Music Analysis 155

Preparing the Foundation 155
Musical Analysis 156
Preparatory Stage 157
Intermediate Stage 159
Advanced Stage 161

Chapter 12: Practical Voice Leading 163

Following the Path of the Masters 163
The Basic Tenets of Voice Leading 164
The Four Types of Motion 164
Using Voice Leading 167
Preparatory Exercise 167
Composition Exercise 168

Chapter 13: Creating Original Chords 169

Beginning Exercise 170
Intermediate Exercise 171
Melody 1 (Treble) 171
Melody 2 (Bass) 171
General Guidelines to Follow 172
Advanced Exercise 173
All Levels: Editing the Composition 175

Chapter 14: Motives 176

The Building Blocks of Music 176

Composition Exercise 178
Beginning Exercise 179
Intermediate Exercise 179
Advanced Exercise 180
Enhancing Your Motives 180
Repetition 181
Rhythm 181
Motives 182

CHAPTER 15: THE RESTRICTED NOTE COMPOSITION 186

Composition Exercise 187
The Note Restrictions 187
Note Values 188
Performance Markings 188
Restricted Note Composition Rules 190

CHAPTER 16: THE ORCHESTRA 192

Instrument Combinations 193
Traditional Combinations 193
Some General Orchestration Guidelines 195
Composition Exercises 196
Beginning Exercise 196
Intermediate Exercise 197
Advanced Exercise 197

CHAPTER 17: COMPOSITIONAL STYLE 199

Beginning Exercise 201
Intermediate Exercise 203
Comparing Mozart and Beethoven 205
Possible Mozart Answers 206
Advanced Exercise 208
Analyzing Music Scores 211

CHAPTER 18: THE PHRASE.. 214

ANTECEDENT AND CONSEQUENT PHRASES 214
COMPOSITION EXERCISES 218
BEGINNING EXERCISE 219
INTERMEDIATE EXERCISE 219
ADVANCED EXERCISE... 219

CHAPTER 19: SCORE PREPARATION................................ 221

HOW TO GET REJECTED IMMEDIATELY 221
SUBMITTING A WORK DESERVING OF ATTENTION 222
CONTEST GUIDELINES 222
COMPUTER GENERATED SCORES.. 222
THE SCORE'S COVER 223
THE FRONT PAGE... 223
THE MUSIC 224
SCORE READABILITY... 225
INSTRUMENTAL PARTS... 225
FORMATTING GUIDELINES... 226
COMPOSITION EXERCISE... 227

ADDITIONAL RESOURCES... 229

THE MUSICAL CORE LECTURE SERIES 229
THE MUSICAL CORE (2019) 229
THE ELEMENTS OF MUSIC COMPOSITION (2018) 230
MUSIC COMPOSITION TECHNIQUE BUILDER (2019)...................... 230
THE CRAFT OF MUSIC COMPOSITION (2020) 231
THE ART OF MUSIC COMPOSITION (2024) 231
UREMUSIC.ORG AND UREMUSIC.COM 232
RECOMMENDED TEXTBOOKS.. 232

Chapter 1: The Genesis

ON COMPOSING MUSIC AND THE CASE FOR MUSIC THEORY

The point is not to take the world's opinion as a guiding star but to go one's way in life and work unerringly, neither depressed by failure nor seduced by applause.

~ Gustav Mahler

Anybody with a desire to compose music can learn the craft with the proper training, but to be a competent composer there must be a blend of craft and art. To be clear, I make a distinction between craft and art. Craft is the technical skill required to compose and notate your musical ideas while art refers to how you apply your craft in creative and meaningful ways.

I began experimenting with writing music when I was eight years old. While I didn't know how to notate my ideas until much later, I was always entranced by the magic of binding musical ideas to manuscript, in taking notes from the air and creating new worlds through the medium of sound.

Before I knew much about composing music, I never felt the blank score was something to fear. The prospect of creating an entirely new musical world was something I undertook with a sort of mystical energy. However, as I continued to develop as a composer, the act of composing took a dangerous turn. I began to fear mistakes and started to wonder if I could possibly compete with the masters of the past. Once I started to care what other people thought about my music, doubt crept in silently. It didn't take long before I was second-guessing every compositional decision I made. Eventually, I stopped trusting my instincts.

Over time, I began to realize that composing is ultimately an individual expression. Mentors can only take you so far, and eventually, you have to branch out on your own and have confidence that your music is infused with both craft and art. Thanks to the technique and knowledge I've acquired over the years, I'm able to work out a composition entirely in my mind and then notate it when it's ready. I still extensively work out my ideas when composing music, but I've reached a level of skill where I'm comfortable and confident in my ability. This doesn't mean that composing no longer poses a challenge, but it does mean that I no longer struggle with the technique of composing a new musical world. This is mostly due to my ability to conceptualize my music before a single note is set to paper, which I aim to help you accomplish through the techniques in this book.

Developing this technique as a composer wasn't an easy process, and more than likely, it won't be an easy process for you either. It took the completion of a bachelor's and master's program in music composition, studying extensively at three different universities, private instruction with some of the most prominent composers of our time, and teaching in a university for me to properly develop my personal technique and learn how to teach others. In essence, it has taken my entire life to reach this point, and my entire life to write this book.

If you want to be a successful composer, you must never stop learning and striving. It is my belief that the moment you think you've made it; stagnation begins to take hold. I don't believe that all aspiring composers need to spend $150,000-plus on an education to learn how to write music effectively. That's why I've taken the time to write a book that is designed to help you become a more effective composer; however, there are still many benefits to a university education that you won't get from this book. Namely, a university education can help you acquire connections in the field of music, work with other performers, and get valuable feedback on your compositions from instructors and peers. Nevertheless, the basic technique and ability to mentally compose music and notate your ideas can be learned from the comfort of home.

Resources that deal with developing music composition techniques are scarce. There are many instructional materials that deal with music theory, counterpoint, form, and voice leading, but few textbooks aim to provide the technical training a composer needs to actually create music.

My hope is that you will build a daily practice regimen that will keep you actively involved in the process of composing music to continually increase your proficiency in the essential "pillars" of music composition. Ultimately, I want to give composers the tools to create music that not only moves the spirit but challenges the mind.

This book isn’t designed to teach you the basics of music composition. You should already understand the basic underlying mechanics of music before undertaking the exercises in this text, which means you should have a basic understanding of how to read music, play an instrument, and some experience writing your own music. However, these exercises also don’t require the prerequisite knowledge of how to create chord progressions, orchestrate, or analyze music. If you are unfamiliar with notes, intervals, scales, triads, and seventh chords, you would benefit from completing *The Musical Core,* available from Kendall Hunt Publishing Company or any number of free theory courses available online.

The Musical Core teaches you about the origins of musical notation, how to read written music, and essential ear training and theory concepts. After completing *The Musical Core*, read through *The Elements of Music Composition* before returning to the *Technique Builder. The Elements of Music Composition* doesn't require much in terms of practical application, and it is a text that can be read straight through to set the stage for the remaining books in the series. After the *Music Composition Technique Builder*, study *The Craft of Music Composition.* Finally, *The Art of Music Composition* serves as a treatise on music that helps you to finalize the process of combining the independent subjects of counterpoint, theory, motivic development, and orchestration.

The Art of Music Composition is a more advanced text that returns to concepts learned in *The Elements of Music Composition.* Using dense language at times, *The Art of Music Composition* requires the successful completion of an undergraduate series in counterpoint, theory, orchestration, and form. If you lack education in these cornerstones, you can study all of the volumes in the Music Composition Technique series to gain the technical knowledge that is obtained in a full undergraduate theory sequence. As of the writing of this book, these additional texts are not yet available. *The Craft of Music Composition* will be available in 2020 and *The Art of Music Composition* by 2024.

The techniques found within this book will take your present ability and build upon it using simple exercises. These technique builders are based on similar assignments that I have provided to my private and university students, but they have been edited to accommodate a wider range of students. Because of this, I have chosen exercises that have been proven to work only with the majority of my students.

A Fugue a Day

Bach reportedly composed a fugue every day before breakfast. Many other composers kept similar routines and practiced basic composition exercises to refine their skill. In Bach's lifetime, music underwent an experimental phase where standards for music were created summarily with each new composition and stemmed from the concept of counterpoint. If you're unfamiliar with the study of counterpoint, it teaches musicians how to combine multiple melodic lines that result in harmony. Using strict rules, composers were taught how to write music based off a fixed melody known as the cantus firmus. By following strict rules for the creation of the counterpoint's melody, students incrementally learned to compose music. The study of counterpoint gave rise to harmony since intervals and chords resulted from the combination of two, three, or more voices.

While counterpoint was a well-established method for helping composers learn to write music, orchestration was barely a subject of discussion. Today, the study of orchestration teaches composers how to combine various instruments to create the most resonant sounds in an orchestra and exploit the uniqueness of instrument timbres to create new sounds. In contrast, Bach would often just give the part to the nearest musician if there wasn't an instrument available. Composers are presently going through a similar period of experimentation; however, music creation tools are much more accessible now and composers also have a wider variety of musical genres compared to any other time in history.

Music composition does have basic structural tendencies, but you can break most any "rule" if you discover a better method for expressing an idea. The trick is learning when and why it's appropriate to break those rules. Moreover, the structural rules should only serve as a starting point for a serious composer. Study music theory so that you can avoid reinventing the wheel. Learn from the masters of the past and stand on their shoulders to take music to new frontiers. Strengthen your technique through daily practice, listen to a wide variety of music, and make music theory your friend. Once you understand the principles behind music theory, you'll begin to see why these theories exist in the first place.

After grasping the reasoning behind the rules and mastering their applications, you can bend or break the "rules" with confidence.

If you are new to composition, you should realize that theory is not just some overly regimented practicum that requires you to follow strict rules in your music. When I was an undergraduate, I despised music theory. I was quite vocal about my disdain, and when one of my mentors asked me how I would work my way out of a particularly thorny chordal trap in my own compositions, I replied that I would simply, "use my ear." After all, isn't the ear good enough?

The not so simple answer is both yes and no. As a composer, you should always trust your ear. However, how can you trust your ear if you don't have the experience to know for certain that your ear is refined and developed enough to recognize poor progressions and voice leading? This may also raise the question of whether the concept of good and bad voice leading really exists. After all, if it sounds good to you, then maybe that's good enough?

One issue with this kind of thinking is that the only way you'll know for certain is if you can first hear music the way the masters of the craft did. Another issue is that before you can make a judgment call on the music of past generations, you first need to understand what the music was based on and how composers arrived at their conclusions. One way to get inside the mind of a composer is to study their music, and music theory provides a quick way to become familiar with the most common chord progressions and structural foundations.

Music theory is not perfect, but it can help you refine your ear to perceive music the way the masters of the past heard music. If you combine music theory with counterpoint, form, and basic composition techniques, you'll be in a great place to accurately judge your own music. I often jokingly say that you have three options available to you if you want to compose music:

1. Create music in a vacuum and pretend that your current understanding of music is based on some preternatural and frankly, supernatural, view of music; therefore, you don't need to learn from anyone.

2. Study thousands of scores and learn how composers of the past created their musical compositions. In essence, learn about your predecessors' accomplishments through hands-on study so that you can create new music and avoid the need to reinvent the wheel. (This one could take some time but *go for it* if you're a vampire who is going to live forever.)

3. Study music theory and benefit from the expertise, decades of analysis, and knowledge acquired from a community of theorists that have dedicated their lives to uncovering the basic mechanical principles of existing music, so that you can create truly original music based on a fundamental understanding of the music that already exists.

This is somewhat of a repeat of a concept I discuss in *The Elements of Music Composition*, but it's such an important point that it can't be left out of a book on music composition technique. Music theory is not an impediment to your craft, but a gift wrapped in gold. Imagine if you could assimilate the knowledge acquired by

Bach, Mozart, Beethoven, Mahler, Stravinsky, Schoenberg, and others to quickly learn what is not "new under the sun?" You would begin your career as a composer knowing what is possible, which enables you to push the development of music composition forward. Theory gives you a reference point to determine if your new composition is revolutionary or based on the theories of a composer who spent a lifetime perfecting their technique. Whether your music ends up being revolutionary or derivative, at least you would know where your music stands if you understand music theory.

If you want to be a composer in the truest sense of the word, you have to create something new. To create something new, you first must understand what already exists. This is where theory comes to rescue. By all means, create the music you love, but dedicate time each day to study music theory and learn how composers of the past solved difficult compositional riddles. You will end up being a better composer for your efforts.

Using This Book

This book contains exercises to help you develop your mind's ear as well as train your aural recognition of basic intervals. The aural recognition exercises were developed for use in several courses at The University of Nevada, Las Vegas. Some of these courses I taught myself while some were taught by other instructors. These exercises have been revised and tested on hundreds of non-music and music majors. Quite simply, the exercises in this book do work, but you have to challenge yourself and push yourself to become better.

For your convenience, this book has been broken up into three parts to help you organize your schedule.

Part I and II includes the technique exercises and suggestions for a Daily Routine and Mirror Exercise that you should complete daily. Part II continues the technique exercises, but also includes some specially formulated 16th century counterpoint exercises to make it easier for you to absorb contrapuntal concepts. A full course in counterpoint is provided in the third volume of the Music Composition Technique Series.

Part III includes some additional reference materials and information that doesn't neatly fit into the Technique Builder course. However, these are useful chapters that should give you some additional insight into music composition, publishing, and preparing your scores.

Each chapter includes a beginning, intermediate, and advanced exercise to choose from. These exercises will improve your skills in different ways and aid your development as a composer. For each chapter, I recommend starting with the beginning exercise and practicing it daily for one week. Next, practice the intermediate exercise for one week. Finally, practice the advanced exercise for at least two weeks or until the end of the month. If this is your first time going through this textbook, momentum is more important than perfection. I suggest on your first run-through to spend no more than two weeks on the advanced exercises. In this fashion, you should complete about one set of techniques per month. On your second run-through, spend as much time as you like on each technique.

You will not love every exercise in this book and some of them may be more suited to your level than others. If you feel that a certain exercise is too simple for you, it's important that you still spend the recommended time working on the exercise during the first run-through. Likewise, don't spend more time on exercises that you find especially enjoyable (spend as much time as you like after your first run-through). Give each exercise an earnest, fair, and equal chance; you may be surprised by the ability of the beginning exercises to develop your skills and perhaps reveal specific weaknesses hidden in your technique.

The beginning exercises have been designed to lay a foundation and condition the neural pathways in your brain. The introductory exercises develop your musical ability in a simple and progressive way, so you have a solid and clean foundation before moving on to the more advanced exercises. After dedicating yourself to the exercises in this book, you will surely notice the profound capability they have to improve your abilities as a composer.

The point of this text is to provide you with a selection of exercises to establish your own practice routine. Just as an athlete routinely trains by running drills or an instrumentalist practices etudes and scales daily, it is essential that composers develop a regimented practice as well. Put in real effort and take the time to understand and complete these exercises. You owe it to yourself to uncover the full potential of your creative abilities by actively engaging in challenging practice regularly.

Once you have completed the exercises in this course, you can choose your favorites and use them to develop your own practice routine. Eventually, just like Bach, you can compose a fugue before breakfast even if there is no time in the day to compose extensively. By doing so, you will keep your brain primed and ready to compose so that when inspiration strikes, you will have the technique and skills to rapidly notate anything you can imagine. More importantly, if you develop the skills taught in this text, you won't need to sit down every day to compose; you will develop the ability to compose anywhere in your spare time. Once your composition is ready, you'll have the technique available to extract your creations from memory and notate your composition in just a few days.

Chapter 2: Daily Routine

CREATING A DAILY COMPOSITION ROUTINE

Inspiration is a guest that does not willingly visit the lazy.

~ *Tchaikovsky*

Before we get into the specific exercises, let's address your daily schedule. Creating a routine ensures that you practice regularly and, as a result, continually develop your skill. It's a cliché, but if something is worth doing, it's worth doing right. So, take the time to prepare your life and schedule to complete the exercises in this textbook properly. If you miss a day, just continue the next day and keep going. Keep in mind that you are bound to struggle the first time you try an exercise, just spend one week each on the beginning and intermediate exercises. Then, spend two weeks on the advanced exercise. For the first time through the exercises, you have worked enough if you have put in four weeks for each technique. It's also okay to spend a few extra days on the advanced exercise during months that have more than 28 days so that you can complete one technique per month.

While the goal is to master each exercise, there is nothing wrong with going through the Technique Builder several times. In fact, it's highly recommended. Each time you go through this textbook, you will find your insights get deeper and your technique improves. Additionally, you can use your initial run-through as an assessment. Keep all of the documents you create from the first run-through, so that when you complete these exercises again, you can see if there is any improvement in your work. If you want to improve more quickly, then all you need to do is *double your failure rate*. People don't succeed until they have failed countless times.

I urge you to set aside as much time as you need to organize your practice sessions and set the stage for a successful training program. If you're starting this textbook in the middle of the month, it's not a bad idea to use the last two weeks to prepare and start at the beginning of the upcoming month. I use the more advanced techniques in this textbook myself, and I try to complete at least two of the exercises per week. On the remaining days, I tend to get inventive and experiment with additional exercises.

Part of establishing a routine involves ensuring that you're always motivated and inspired to work. I often need to address this issue with my students. As a student (we never stop being students) I also struggle with bouts of creative lethargy. I'm not immune, so I feel motivation serves as an important aspect of not only this course, but of becoming a successful musician and a well-adjusted human.

You may find that many of the ideas in the textbook are applicable to areas of your life beyond composition. That's the beauty of music instruction; it helps you to get organized and stick to your goals. The discipline gained from studying music seeps into other areas of your life in a positive way. Music instruction also serves as an important reminder that if you keep working, you can master any skill.

Take the time to reflect on what you're trying to accomplish as a composer. Even if you find it difficult to compose over the next few months, this chapter can help you to make real progress in your compositions. Your attitude toward writing and working daily in general may also begin to shift. So, let's get ready to complete these composition exercises.

Motivation

"Composing music is hard work."

~ John Williams

Let's be clear about one thing: music composition requires a significant investment of emotional energy, physical energy, and time. It's not for the faint of heart. I've worked jobs that have required physical labor, jobs that have required significant mental labor, and jobs that have required a bit of both. All work can drain you of your resources and energy. Don't think for a moment because you are simply sitting at a desk composing that it isn't hard work. Luckily, composing is also one of the most rewarding callings you can undertake. If you're a composer, no amount of rejection or failure will keep you from writing music. Even so, when you produce music on a daily basis, it can become difficult to find the motivation to write every day.

One of my earlier instructors worked with me to develop habits with the goal of composing on a regular schedule, and these habits were rooted primarily in an emotional response to writing. My instructor asked whether I felt guilty on the days when I didn't compose. When I answered that I felt bad about not working on music every day, he said, "Well, that's a start."

I don't think that using guilt as a way to motivate yourself to compose is necessarily the healthiest method, even if it does work in the beginning stages. Aside from the psychological implications of that kind of thinking, I feel it's important to move past those initial emotional motivators that may propel you to create new works. It's far more useful to develop consistent habits that make it possible to stick to a routine.

But, let's take a step back for a moment so that I can tell you about my own experiences with motivation. The more I composed using an emotional barometer, the more I realized that it was not an effective way of dealing with the achievement giants named *motivation* and *inspiration*. I bring this up because many musicians place their value as a person on how much they worked that day, how well a performance went, or whether they mastered a new skill in a practice session. It's important to realize that you may be a composer or musician, but there is also a tremendous value put on the kind of person you are. We are more than what we provide or produce, even if it sometimes feels like the only thing that matters to the world is production. Having said all of this, guilt was the right motivator for me when I started composing. I'm grateful my instructor knew me well enough to give me the right push. Since then, I've found more efficient and healthy ways to establish a routine, and I'd like to share some of my findings with you.

We all have something that drives us to create music. As mentioned previously, for the longest time, my motivation was charged by a feeling that has less to do with the actual merit of my work and more to do with a rather simplistic idea of just working harder. The theory was that working more will somehow result in the accomplishment of my goals. Unfortunately, as a motivating factor, working for the sake of working can be hard to maintain. The problem is that *working harder only produces more work, it doesn't necessarily produce good work.*

When it comes to motivation, it's important to realize we all have our own ways of getting into the right state of mind to compose. Using guilt slowly eroded the original reason I wanted to write music — to express ideas, thoughts, tell a story, and create musical worlds that were meaningful to me. I finally arrived at a point where it didn't matter what anyone else thought. Forming a meaningful connection to my musical creations offers a good enough reason to continue writing on a daily basis.

Ultimately, relying upon socials constructs like guilt as the basis for writing is not a suitable long-term strategy. It borders on pathological thinking, and it can end up creating additional anxiety about the composing process. It may work in the beginning stages, but as you develop and become more serious about writing, you must find a more sustainable source of inspiration.

Your motivation for writing music is personal, but I ask that you take a few moments to think about your reasons for deciding to become a composer. If you think you will do this later, you probably won't. In a moment, I'm going to ask you to think about your reasoning with a short assignment so start preparing yourself to complete this task and don't take it lightly.

Arnold Schoenberg mentions in his *Harmonielehre* that there is a certain usefulness in movement. He refers to an old puzzle that can essentially be solved in two ways: you can shake the puzzle, and eventually the pieces will fall into place; or, you can be methodical about it and try to force your will on the puzzle. According to Schoenberg, both options tend to yield results. The underlying message is that movement in itself is important, and it's based on something he observed in his students. When his students kept moving, they eventually made progress. So, let's start moving now with a little assignment.

Whether you are just starting out or an accomplished writer, the reason we do anything is as important as the act itself. It's crucial to firmly understand why you're devoting yourself to composition. Set time aside now and figure out what music and music composition means to you. Your definition can, and likely should, change with time. But, it's important to create a starting point so that we can look back in the future and see how far we've come. This serves as a valuable motivator to remind yourself years from now why you started to compose music in the first place. If you don't write this down, you may very well forget.

Consider this your first assignment: refine and articulate your purpose for composing music. Write down at least one reason. Take a few moments or even a day to think about your answer.

Maybe your answer will be something like the following statement:

"I compose music because I must give expression to my feelings, just as I talk because I must give utterance to my thoughts."

~ Sergei Rachmaninoff

Once you think you have the answer, ask yourself another important question: if you achieved this purpose, is there a deeper purpose would you like to achieve?

Repeat this cycle a few times over the next few days until you arrive at an answer that really resonates with you. (Yes, this is a multi-day event, and you seeing how your answer changes can be enlightening.) If you write something down and don't feel any excitement, then you haven't yet reached the core of what drives you. Keep going until you have a revelation. Fair warning though, some students complete this exercise and find that they don't want to pursue music. If that's what you learn from this exercise, then this book has just paid for itself by saving you time and effort. The more likely scenario is that you will discover some hidden desire within you that will fuel you through your composition studies. No matter the outcome, what you discover may surprise you. Once you write down your reason for composing music, keep it in a highly visible place. Make it your mantra and repeat it daily.

When you come across periods of low motivation, you can revisit this statement and remind yourself why you started composing. You'll find that your reasons for composing music might change over your lifetime but having a clear reason for why you're composing can help you get through the hills and valleys frequently found along the road to becoming a better composer.

Maybe you don't have an issue with motivation. This may be true for the time being; but, if you continue to compose regularly, there will be days when your passion and drive aren't enough to get you to sit down and write. This is when good habits become essential. A regular routine will enable you to continue working even on the days when you don't feel like doing anything at all. If you want to succeed, natural talent and inherited ability simply aren't enough. You will need to work more intelligently than everyone else.

The key to cultivating motivation and fueling it through concentrated effort is maintaining a positive mentality. It's important to realize that you are not a victim of your mood or your circumstances. No matter what is going on in your personal or professional life, the news on the television or social media, or the many busy errands that overwhelm you, finding time to practice your composition technique each day has to be a priority if you want to be a composer — no excuses.

Outside distractions are just noise that prevent you from focusing on your goals. Assuming you are in good health and have the ability to work daily toward your goals, you can find a way to carve out 15 minutes each day to complete at least a single exercise.

The good news about motivation is that you don’t actually need motivation to work toward a goal. *Feeling* like doing something and having the *ability* to do something are two different things. You can still work if you feel completely uninspired. If you sit down for an hour and feel you have accomplished nothing, you’re thinking about the process the wrong way. Any work results in small shards of progress that can set the stage for future work. Just showing up to work is a good start, and it is the beginning of progress. After a couple days, weeks, or even months of showing up for work, your mind will finally relent and give way to focus. Over time, your mind will begin to recognize this time slot as your composing time, and ideas will start flowing every day like clockwork.

I realize that this goes against the intuitive and flexible nature of many composers. What is important to realize is that motivation doesn't have to be an elusive spirit. You can tame motivation and make it appear on time if you schedule your routine. It can take significant time to take effect; but eventually, you'll find that setting aside an hour each day where you will not be disturbed will become an important part of your process. This doesn't mean you can't be driven to motivation at other times in the day. It simply deepens the well of motivation during your daily composition hours.

Inspiration

"The great composer does not set to work because he is inspired, but becomes inspired because he is working. Beethoven, Wagner, Bach and Mozart settled down day after day to the job in hand with as much regularity as an accountant settles down each day to his figures. They didn't waste time waiting for inspiration."

~ Ernest Newman (English music critic and musicologist)

Once you have your motivation under control, you need to think about how to manage your muse. I stand by my statement that you need to develop composition technique. This way, when inspiration hits, you have the tools through which to effectively channel your ideas. However, what should be understood is that inspiration doesn't have to be some elusive concept that only comes to you when the planets align, and you are in the right frame of mind to receive a melody from on high.

There are many things you can do to bring inspiration on-demand into the here and now. The composer, Philip Glass, for instance, uses a daily schedule as a way to force his creative thoughts into a specified time slot. He schedules his inspiration, and he actively puts ideas on hold if they come at any other time of the day. Whether or not you force your inspiration into a particular time slot is up to you. But it is a good idea to have a set time each day where you are open to inspiration, so that your mind becomes accustomed to this schedule. If you choose to suppress your inspiration and make it come to you at a time and schedule of your choosing, there are some techniques you can use to ensure you don't lose any great ideas.

Inspiration Corralling Tools

Composition Notebook: Keep a composition notebook or a voice recorder/smartphone on hand. If you get an idea for a new melody or composition, write it down or make a quick recording. Download a voice recording or notation app specifically for this purpose to keep your ideas organized.

Journal: Commit yourself to keeping a journal; whether it be a record of your everyday happenings, a dream journal logging the visions that come to you in sleep, or an emotional outlet for your encounters throughout the day. Pick an entry (or several) and translate your musings into music. Or, for an even greater challenge, journal entirely in music from the start, substituting notation for words. What melody would you write to celebrate a job promotion? What motive comes to you when expressing life troubles? How would you notate getting stuck in rush-hour traffic?

The composer John Cage sent his audience out into traffic to listen to the sounds of the street using a pre-scheduled route. Turn this on its head by actually composing the sounds of traffic to test your limits and improve your ability to compose anything you can imagine. How is this related to a journal you ask? A journal can be literary in nature, but it can also simply be a random collection of melodies or rhythms. It doesn't mean you will attempt to compose a piece based on these ideas; but remember, a mind in motion tends to stay in motion. Get weird and think up all kinds of strange ideas for composing music. Again, you don't have to act on these ideas. The simple process of coming up with these ideas will increase your creativity. I'm not suggesting you compose a piece based on the sounds of traffic or a walk in the woods as a serious attempt at composition but putting in the effort to transcribe these sounds will help improve your technique.

Enjoy Artwork: Look for art that appeals to you. Think about how you could turn art into a music composition. Search for ways to musically express the things that are going on around you every day. It doesn't matter if you use the ideas, just as long as you're maintaining an active and vibrant imagination for composing. Art and music have long been connected. Historically, movements in art tended to inspire the related musical movements and styles.

Get Moving: Go for a walk and allow yourself to become absorbed in your thoughts. Sometimes a change of scenery can help you come up with new ideas. Inspiration comes as the result of being exposed to new ideas and events. Stay active in your life and seek new forms of inspiration to help you prepare for your next composition. I find that a car ride, time outdoors, books, or movies can inspire ideas for my next project. Sometimes I just need to sit and vegetate to recover my energy, but even in those low moments, I'm thinking about my next steps. Depending on my mood, I'll even go running and let thoughts come to me.

Schedule Time: Perhaps most importantly, set aside a time and place each day where you can compose completely undisturbed. Turn off the television; silence your phone; take a vacation from your social media site or game that might lure you away from your work. Create a separate user account on your computer solely for composing to minimize distractions. Scheduling time is the basis for The Composing Hour, which I discuss in detail in the upcoming pages.

Finally, I'll end with a quote from Shostakovich taken from the text *Testimony: The Memoirs of Dmitri Shostakovich.*

I'll admit that writing doesn't always come, but I'm totally against walking around and looking at the sky when you're experiencing a block, waiting for inspiration to strike you. Tchaikovsky and Rimsky-Korsakov didn't like each other and agreed on very few things, but they were of one opinion on this: you had to write constantly. If you can't write a major work, write minor trifles. If you can't write at all, orchestrate something. I think Stravinsky felt the same thing.

The basic message here is that you have to write often to be a composer and develop as a composer. However, writing music can come in several forms. This also seems to go against my belief that taking a walk can be a good way to get inspired. Once you develop the ability to compose in your mind, then you can, in fact, take a walk and create the beginnings of a new work. If taking a walk worked for Beethoven, it's certainly a valid technique for any composer.

Write music every day that you can. Work to improve your technique during the times that writing doesn't always come. While this course is initially intended to create a segment of time that you sit down to work every day, in the end, you want to reach the point where the techniques in this book are used for those times that "writing doesn't always come."

I'll also briefly point out that Shostakovich was referring to composers who had already gone through significant training, so writing minor trifles might not be the best option for a composer who is still developing their technique. Since you are currently going through a training process, your daily work should aim to develop your inner ear so that you don't have to sit at a desk to write music. Once you develop your inner ear, you'll be free to compose anywhere with a small notebook to jot down ideas for aiding in memory recall.

Chapter 3: The Composing Hour

"The joy of music should never be interrupted by a commercial."

~ Leonard Bernstein

Technology provides an incredible platform for information and communication. Of course, it can also be used for disinformation and isolation. But when you need to focus your mind on work, technology typically serves as a distraction. You cannot multitask while studying and creating music; it requires 100% of your devoted concentration. This brings us to the concept of *The Composing Hou*r. This hour is a time for you that you should aim to set aside every day to develop your technique and skill.

The following suggestions should place you in the right frame of mind to work. These methods have been successful for me and my students throughout the years, so give them a try and modify the schedule to fit your lifestyle and time constraints. Just keep in mind that short, concentrated bursts of focused effort can be just as effective as slow and disjointed work that takes all day.

Break up your daily composition hour into four 15-minute components. Set a timer for each component so that you know when to move on to the next component. Over time, you'll find that 15 minutes isn't enough time, and you will feel a desire to increase your time. Avoid the temptation to increase the time you're spending on each component. When you finish with your hour, you can return and spend additional time on any of these components. Keep moving but stop working before you get bored to ensure you maintain momentum. This is one of the greatest techniques for increasing motivation and inspiration, and it can take you through some rough patches in your life. You can allocate more time for your routine if this is your second time completing this course, but only if you were successful in sitting down each day for one hour during the initial cycle. When I say each day, I'm referring to five or six days a week. If you push for seven, you may get burnt out too quickly.

Important: you should already have all of the materials for your composing hour set up and ready to go. Do not waste any time from your composing hour finding the documents you need. They should be laid out on your desk or available electronically so that you make every second of your composing hour count. You will find that the composing hour involves very little actual composition. Instead, the goal is to complete your daily training and get you primed to compose music once your hour is up. Once you develop your inner ear, you can reduce time spent in your composing hour. You may even find that eventually, you can eliminate technique entirely and just spend your time composing music. However, depending on your starting point, expect this to take a few years. Yes, I know. Nobody wants to hear something will take a few years, but time will fly, and you will eventually regret not taking the time now to develop skills that will benefit you for a lifetime.

While it's not required, it's recommended that you invest in a keyboard to more easily complete some of these exercises and to get your starting pitches. If you took *The Musical Core* course, then you already know how to identify notes on the piano. If you didn't take this course, you can use any online keyboard or learn the basic notes on the piano from any number of online sources. UreMusic.org also includes plenty of free basic articles that I wrote in my graduate program. The articles detail many aspects of performance, theory, orchestration, and counterpoint.

The Composing Hour Schedule

Remember, each component in your composing hour should be practiced for a total of 15 minutes. Don't exceed an hour your first time through this text. Give yourself no more than three hours for any successive attempts. You shouldn't spend more than three hours because you need to leave some time to compose music in your day. These exercises are only intended to serve as short exercises that will help you continually develop your technique. All of the techniques in this book are designed to be completed in 15 minutes or less. Make sure you set a timer for each segment so that you don't go over your allotted time. It's not a bad idea to supplement the *Technique Builder* with the *Craft of Music Composition* starting with your second time around.

Ear Training: A Daily Routine and Mirror Exercise are available to help you develop and improve your ear. Practice these daily (at least five days per week). Begin your routine with these exercises and aim to sing through them in your allotted time. If you don't get through the entire routine, stop and try again the next day. However, it is very important that you move slowly and learn to sing these routines on pitch. If it takes you a few weeks to learn these routines, it's okay. Take care to avoid making mistakes. The brain does not differentiate between mistakes and intention. If you make a mistake, the brain will see it as a potential option for the future. Then, you will need to practice a section several more times to override that mistake. If you need help with the Daily Routines, you should learn to play these on a piano or keyboard. As an alternative, you can enter them into a notation program and play them back. While the Daily Routines are included in this book, the print may be too small for many readers. For this reason, you may also download them from the following link:

https://mailchi.mp/5f3eab74b0ad/uremusic

Editing: Spend time editing and analyzing your old compositions. Editing is a process you can complete even when you barely have the energy to lift your arms. You may find that as you edit, you will begin to get excited about creating new compositions. Take notes, mark up your score, draw graphs to indicate the shape of the melody and bass line. Examine your music and be highly critical so that when you have time to sit down later, you will know what needs to be changed.

Brainstorming: Brainstorming may sometimes turn into free time where you simply sit and let your mind wander. This time could be used to brainstorm new ideas, do something different, or simply let your mind wander. You don't have to write anything down during these periods. However, I recommend jotting down some random ideas — they may prove valuable at a later time. Use your brainstorming sessions to improve your imagination. Mentally imagine a performance of a new work, write down ideas for a new composition, compose a simple melody or motive. Don't worry if your ideas are any good. You can brainstorm musical ideas or literary ideas. The important thing is that you work actively and avoid making judgments about your creations during this time.

Composition Technique: End each composing hour with the techniques that are included in this text. If it's your first time through this course, then you should go through the techniques in order. If you're going through this a second time, then you can choose the techniques you want to include each day. But, make your decisions the night before to prepare and be ready to make the most out of your composing hour.

As a reminder, you should work your way through the text and work on each technique for one month. The beginning and intermediate exercises should last you one week each. The advanced exercises should be practiced for two weeks. The exercises can be practiced daily ***no matter how you feel that day.*** Once you've gone through the textbook, choose the exercises you like most and create a personalized daily practice routine.

After your composing hour, you are free to revisit revelations from the hour. You may wish to start composing, get ready for work/bed, or generally get on with your day/night. The important thing is that you invest an hour of your day in yourself so that you continue to develop as a composer and become a more effective artist. The time you spend developing your inner ear will be greatly rewarded with increased ability and enjoyment from the process of composing.

Routine Triggers

Create 'triggers' that signal to your body and mind that you're ready to work. The most significant hurdle many people experience before undertaking a task, especially a creative task, is the simple act of getting started. A trigger, which should be simple and easy to perform on any given day, is not overwhelming in and of itself. When consistently used to initiate your composing time, triggers can positively act as a catalyst to set you in motion.

Examples of triggers:

The following triggers are not meant to be comprehensive. Use these as a guide to create your own triggers based on how you live and work.

Coffee/Tea/Water: Grab a glass of water or your caffeinated, decaffeinated, or uncaffeinated beverage of choice and take it to your desk, kitchen table, or quiet corner. Enjoy a few sips and begin your composing hour. Gradually, you will associate this small ritual with writing music and will find it easier to get started each day if you habitually stick with the same routine.

Shower: Take a shower, get ready for the day, and sit down to write before doing anything else. Often, if you write directly after a shower, you will find that your mind starts to become active while taking your shower. Also, as a bonus, you'll be less likely to smell.

Other Triggers: Alarms (ie. Set an alarm for the same time every day when you will compose); Meals (ie. Commit to compose after dinner every day); and Quick Chores (ie. After taking care of the dishes or walking the dog, sit down to compose.)

Think of your compositional practice session as a routine task that you must do every day, no different from your other daily obligations.

Don't Forget the Importance of Breaks!

The Harvard Business Review and the National Institute on Aging have cited numerous studies that show overworking accelerates age-related memory loss and a decline in fluid intelligence. The Mayo Clinic has also cited several studies that show sitting for long periods of time contributes to many health issues. Even without the research to support active breaks, it's common-sense that moving is good for you. So, Move!

If you are going to apply yourself fully to a job, creative or otherwise, the importance of breaks can't be stressed enough. Once you complete your composing hour, take a five-minute break, making sure to move. In general, you should aim to move for 5 minutes at least once per hour. In my breaks, I often complete pushups, jumping jacks, or simply stand up and stretch. Yes, I really use the composing hour every day when possible. It's a critical part of my routine, but life tends to get in the way and I am no longer in desperate need of development. Once you have a suitable level of technique, you can reduce the number of days that you devote to your composing hour, too. However, while training, you should aim to make this hour a mandatory part of your day.

If you're a composer who writes for long stretches of time, make sure to always incorporate active breaks into your sessions. Breaks will help you maintain a fresh perspective, especially at the completion of a task. You'll find that when working with creative material, stepping back for a slight intermission allows you to return to your task with fresh eyes (or ears). You may also be pleasantly surprised to feel yourself itching to get back to work on most days.

Part I: Technique

You have now made it to Part I of the *Technique Builder*. As a reminder, if this is your first time through the textbook, aim to complete every exercise in order and spend approximately one month per technique using a 1-1-2 weekly schedule for the beginning, intermediate, and advanced exercises. Complete your composing hour daily. The technique builder serves as a 15-minute segment of this complete daily one-hour routine.

Summary of Exercises

1. Use the composing hour to complete your four segments:
    - Ear training
    - Editing
    - Brainstorming
    - Technique
2. Each segment should last about 15 minutes, and you should set a timer. The goal is to finish while you still want to keep working.
3. For the ear training portion, you may wish to invest in the physical textbook so that you can have a hard copy of the daily routines and mirror exercise available to you. You can also copy the routines by hand, which would be a great exercise in itself.
4. **1-1-2:** Spend 1 week on the beginning exercises, 1 week on the intermediate exercises, and 2 weeks (or until the end of the month) on the advanced exercises.
5. Complete the composing hour at least 5 times per week. You can complete it daily if you don't think you'll get burnt out. Use your judgment and take a day off if you need, but you should still "show up" during your time and read, compose, or get caught up on other work.

Composing Effectively

Since one of the aims of this text is to help you become organized and write more efficiently, your composition technique exercises often focus on helping you develop a more active and effective musical mind. This is accomplished through exercises that develop your ability to work with multiple independent lines. Provided you know how to read music (an essential requirement to becoming a composer), you should be able to complete most of these exercises. If you don't know how to read music, there are plenty of resources available online.

I also keep a list of useful resources that you can use at UreMusic.com in the "Resources" section. My introductory theory and ear training text used in colleges is also available through Kendall Hunt Publishing Company. Look for *The Musical Core* if you're interested. This book starts with the basics of identifying note names and has several drills to help you master fundamental theory and aural skills. By the end of the course, you'll learn about modes, scales, key signatures, triads, and seventh chords. The course also helps you to develop your ear.

Composition Exercises

Keep in mind that the *spirit* of the exercises that are available in Part I should become a part of your daily routine for the rest of your life. This means that while the exercises may change or be replaced with actual composition, you should try to maintain your composing hour if it works for you. Completing these exercises daily will help keep your mind active and prime you for thinking about your music for the rest of the day. While you will need to refine these exercises as you develop, they serve as an excellent starting point for establishing your technique. Always keep in mind that the best way to become a better composer is to compose music; however, if you can create a daily one-hour routine that you can easily complete, you'll get more out of your time spent composing.

Remember, the goal is to create a sustainable daily practice routine that you can complete no matter how hectic your life may become. The goal isn't to regiment a 12-hour composing session that limits your creativity; rather, the goal is to create an exercise routine to continually develop your technique and gradually increase your skill. When composing serious music, I believe there needs to be some flexibility in your scheduling. While the composing hour ensures you get the minimum practicing in to sustain and improve your abilities, ultimately, composing is how you become a better problem solver and composer. Technique is simply there to help you gain an increased ability to mentally imagine your compositions.

The Technique Builder sets the stage for you to improve through daily practice of concepts. The initial exercises will guide you with musical examples, but once you complete each technique the first time through, you should have the ability to start creating your own exercises based on your unique challenges. It may be tempting to start off creating your own exercises right off the bat, but it's extremely important you start with the exercises in this textbook first. The exercises have been selected for their effectiveness in building a strong foundation, so please work through them before going off on your own.

Don't forget to practice your Daily Routines and Mirror Exercises during the Ear Training portion of The Composing Hour. Here is the rundown of how to coordinate the techniques along with the ear training materials.

Start with the Daily Routine followed immediately by the mirror exercise associated with the current technique. Then, move on to editing, brainstorming, and finally complete the technique for the current chapter.

	Ear Training 15 Minutes	Editing 15 Minutes	Brainstorming 15 Minutes	Technique 15 Minutes
Month 1	DR1+ME1	Pages 33-34	Pages 33-34	Chapter 4
Month 2	DR2+ME2	Pages 33-34	Pages 33-34	Chapter 5
Month 3	DR3+ME3,4	Pages 33-34	Pages 33-34	Chapter 6
Month 4	DR4+ME5,6	Pages 33-34	Pages 33-34	Chapter 7
Month 5	DR5+ME7,8	Pages 33-34	Pages 33-34	Chapter 8
Month 6	DR6+ME9,10	Pages 33-34	Pages 33-34	Chapter 9
Month 7	DR7+ME11,12	Pages 33-34	Pages 33-34	Chapter 10

DR = Daily Routine
ME = Mirror Exercise

Download the workbook, schedule, and audio files at the following link:

https://mailchi.mp/5f3eab74b0ad/uremusic

Chapter 4: The Rhythmic Motor

PUSHING MUSIC FORWARD

The heart of a music is its rhythm.

~ Wynton Marsalis

Rhythm drives our music, and it surrounds us everywhere we go. The rhythm of your heartbeat, the sound of people walking down the street, and even the rhythm of pattering rain can all serve as inspiration for a musical work.

As a composer, you can use the world as a model for your compositions. Take anything of interest to use as inspiration in a potential new composition. If you walk outside in the summer and hear cicadas in surround sound, it may inspire a new piece for you to compose. The repetitive knocking of a woodpecker might inspire the rhythm in your next composition. To take these abstract sounds and realize them in concrete music notation requires a certain amount of skill and a good enough memory to remember the rhythm (or maybe a recording device). Producing effective music requires a solid understanding of how to create remarkable and memorable rhythms. While using nature as the basis for a composition is fine, make sure you try to employ the concepts learned in *The Elements of Music Composition* to create work with a purpose.

Rhythm serves as the engine that drives your composition forward. Without rhythm, your musical composition would lack focus and structure. Many composers have an excellent ability to weave harmonic and melodic tapestries, but their music lacks a rhythmic pulse to propel the piece forward.

The rhythm technique is not designed to help you improve your ability to write rhythms, but it does create the foundation to mentally envision your compositions. I've found the best way to start the process of composing music completely in your mind is to begin with simple rhythms.

Rhythm is useless if you can't notate it in a playable form, and you should be able to notate basic rhythms easily. If you're not yet able to notate rhythms, it's time to begin working on this ability. It's one of the most essential elements of music, and most people are able to imitate and clap basic rhythms even without the skill to notate what they are hearing. While beyond the scope of this text, you can use the following process if you're having trouble notating rhythms:

1. Clap a random rhythm or listen to the rhythm from the melody of a favorite song.
2. Notate what you *think* you're hearing. Notice I said 'think', which implies that what you are hearing may not actually be what is being played. This happens often with younger musicians, where they think they hear a rhythm but fail to notate it correctly. The solution for this is more practice.
3. Use a metronome to play back the rhythm to see if it sounds right. If the rhythm doesn't match what you hear, keep trying until you get the rhythm right. You can even use a notation program to check your rhythms and have them played back for you, but try to write out the initial rhythms by hand to put more intention into your exercise.
4. Return to Step 1, repeat this process, and continually push yourself to notate increasingly complex rhythms with accuracy.

When I was teaching at a lab school affiliated with The University of Arizona, I was given the opportunity to work with under-represented children. One of my classes was a course devoted to teaching middle school children how to compose music. The students came to the class with no knowledge of how to read or notate music. With the help of technology, I had them composing basic musical works by the end of the year. It wasn't an easy task, but I accomplished it by beginning with the simplest element of music – rhythm.

Once the students could notate rhythms, they could use technology to move the notes up or down and create pleasing melodies they enjoyed. Rhythm served as the basis for their ability to compose melodies. Students were able to notate their rhythms in a music notation program and move the notes up and down in the computer program to find the pitch they wanted. I taught them basic concepts, such as how to make their melodies use mostly stepwise motion, and if they did use something other than stepwise motion, to resolve any leaps (anything larger than a third) in the opposite direction. I also instructed them to make sure their melodies begin and end on the same pitch. Beginning and ending on the same pitch isn't required for a good melody, but this was an appropriate restriction to teach the concept of tonality to younger children.

I also taught using an oversimplification of voice leading, but it allowed the students to get excited when they listened to their melodies and composed music that made sense melodically. This allowed them to begin the process of creating melodies. But, more importantly, it got the students moving. It seems Newton's first law also applies to middle school students with a slight modification: a *mind* at rest tends to stay at rest, and a *mind* in motion tends to stay in motion. *Let's be honest, this maxim also applies to most sentient beings.* The students who went on to a second year could create melodies based off what they heard internally.

With time, most people can learn to notate rhythms, but there are two skills that need to be mastered. The first skill involves improving your basic ability to memorize a rhythm that you see or hear. The second skill is becoming proficient at finding the pulse in the rhythm so that you can then notate what you're hearing. We are going to focus on the first skill. The second skill is a skill that should be worked on with a private instructor, a friend who can read music and play rhythms for you, or a software program that focuses on dictation exercises.

For your first three exercises, you will be using *Exercise 1.1.* I suggest you copy this exercise by hand or input it into a notation program and keep it in a book of exercises. Copying music by hand is one of the best ways to gain familiarity with a piece of music. The mind naturally tries to play back the notes as you write them on the page, and this helps you improve your musical acuity. You can even create copies of the exercise to track your progress. Write the current date down for each attempt, and then note any issues you encountered while completing the exercise.

Exercise 1.1 (MM=60)

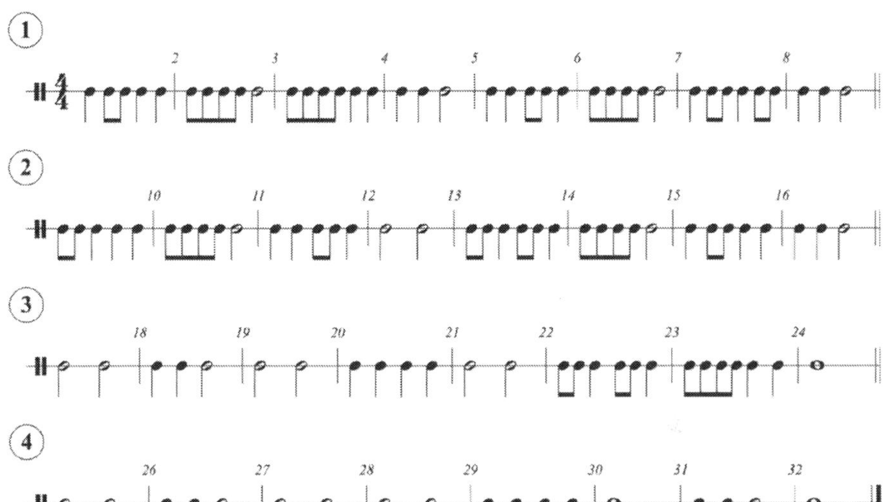

Beginning Stage

1 Week; 15 Minutes Per Day

Practice the beginning exercise for an entire week. Even if it is still difficult after a week, move on to the intermediate exercise. Remember, we are not aiming for perfection. When you go through this book a second, third, or fourth time, you will likely find that you have improved. Improvement and movement are the ultimate goals since this will help you improve throughout the rest of your life. With steady practice you may eventually perfect these exercises, but just do as much as your current ability permits today. For those of you that are advanced, you may be tempted to skip this initial exercise. Feel free to do that on the second time around, but this first time is intended to set the stage for further work. Please do not skip this exercise, it's only 15 minutes out of your day. This exercise builds the foundation for more complex work, and it cannot be skipped if you want to see results.

Select the first eight-bar rhythm from *Example 1.1.* Clap, tap, or sing the rhythm on a single pitch. Then, close your eyes and try to hear the rhythm clearly in your mind. You're only allowed to rehearse this rhythm one time before attempting a mental recall. If you don't memorize the rhythm the first time, mentally play as much of it as you can and then clap the rhythm again. Complete this action for the duration of your 15-minute period. The goal is to try and memorize more of the rhythm each time as you continue to improve.

If you easily memorize the first eight-bar rhythm, feel free to move on to the second eight-bar rhythm. For those of you that are able to memorize all four eight-bar rhythms on the first day, attempt to recall these rhythms on day two *without cheating* and looking at the notation. If you can do that as well, then it's time to start writing your own rhythms to memorize. If that's too advanced, purchase a book of rhythms that get progressively more complex and start memorizing those.

Exercise 1.1 includes four eight-bar rhythms you can use to get started. Notice that there is a double bar line in measure 8, 16, and 24. Measure 31 uses a final bar line. These double and final bar lines are used to indicate the ends of each rhythm.

There are only four rhythms to allow you the chance to take the first day to learn how to complete this exercise. This way you can use the second through fifth day to mentally practice the rhythms. I recommend practicing this exercise all seven days of the week if you find that you are still having trouble after day five.

As you progress through this first exercise, you can skip forward and check out the *Exercise Tips* section at the end of this chapter. There are tips to modify this exercise and make it more difficult, as well as some tips to help you if you're struggling.

Beginning Exercise

1. Select one of the rhythms from *Example 1.1.*
2. Clap or sing the rhythm on a single pitch.
3. Close your eyes and try to mentally replay the rhythm in your mind.
    a. If you can't mentally replay the entire rhythm from memory, go back to Step 2.
    b. If you can mentally replay the entire rhythm, return to Step 1 and complete the process with the next rhythm.
    c. If you memorize all of the rhythms, create more rhythms and memorize those for the remainder of your time this week.

Intermediate Stage

1 Week; 15 Minutes Per Day

The intermediate exercise is designed to build upon the beginning exercise. In this exercise, you'll be expanding your ability to memorize rhythm, which is arguably a very difficult concept to master. By this point, you should have the ability to play all four rhythms in the beginning exercise. If you are still having trouble playing the beginning exercises, then pick the two rhythms that you are having the easiest time playing and use those for the duration of this level.

At the intermediate level, you're starting to develop a very powerful inner voice that can help you compose music entirely in your head. This exercise is simple, but you should find that the inner voice gets clearer over the course of the month. Eventually, your ability to mentally recall rhythms will become so pronounced that playing the rhythm of a piece without the need for an external instrument will become possible. While notation programs are very useful for helping you hear the basic structure of your piece, they are not as fast, flexible, or creative as your mind.

This exercise will take the initial four rhythms and combine them until you are able to mentally recall the entire exercise. This time around, you might not be able to memorize the entire rhythm from measure 1-32. That's okay, the next time you complete the Technique Builder, you should be better equipped to handle the rhythms. Spend one week on this, and you will see how the rest of the exercises build upon this one initial set of rhythms.

I'm going to attempt to paint you a picture of how these exercises will benefit you in the future. When you read a novel, it's very likely that you get wrapped up in the storyline and can begin to see the features of the characters in the book. If you get really absorbed, you may even begin to feel like you're in the storyline and you can see all of the characters actions play out. You're still aware of your surroundings, but you are intensely occupied with the storyline and watching it unfold in your mind's eye. Hearing music can provide you with the same sort of experience. The only difference is that for most of our lives we act as recipients of music, where with literary tales, we actively engage our minds and visualize the story. The intermediate exercise is designed to engage your mind and help you develop your inner ear, which is something you likely have never attempted to accomplish before.

One of the things I have asked you to do is to close your eyes during the recall portion of the exercise. It's important that you follow that instruction. Closing your eyes is one way to create a small bit of sensory deprivation. By reducing the need for your brain to process visual information, your auditory senses become more acute. While memorizing the rhythms helps you to increase your musical memory, the real benefit of this exercise is in helping you to develop the clarity of the sounds you hear mentally. Over time, your inner ear will grow increasingly capable of hearing music internally.

For this exercise, you're going to attempt to memorize as much of the 32-bar melody as you can. Do it progressively. First, memorize rhythm one. Then, connect rhythm one and two together in a single 16-bar rhythm. Next, connect one, two, and three in a 24-bar rhythm. Finally, connect all four rhythms together in a single 32-bar rhythm. Again, if you don't get to the final rhythm, that's okay. That simply means you have more room to grow the next time around. If you are easily able to accomplish this exercise, then get a book of rhythms and attempt to memorize increasingly complex and longer rhythms. In many ways, starting with rhythm is harder than starting with melody. However, rhythm lays the groundwork for the remaining exercises, so it's important you concentrate and memorize as much as you can within your limited 15-minute period.

Intermediate Exercise

1. Clap the first 8-bar rhythm.
2. Close your eyes and try to mentally replay the rhythm in your mind.
    a. If you cannot replay the entire rhythm from memory, go back to Step 1.
    b. If you *can* mentally replay the entire rhythm, move to Step 3.
3. Clap and rehearse the first two rhythms without taking a break in between each rhythm. So, you should clap measures 1-16 without stopping.*
4. Close your eyes and mentally replay measures 1-16. Move on to Step 5 when you can do this.*
5. Go back and rehearse the first three rhythms without taking a break between each rhythm. Perform measures 1-24 without stopping. *
6. Close your eyes and mentally replay measures 1-24. Move on to Step 7 when you can do this.*
7. Continue the process to include rhythm 4 so that you are mentally recalling the entire exercise. Once you complete this step, move on to Step 8.*
8. Attempt to mentally recall all of rhythm 4 at the start of your next session. Once you can do this, spend the rest of the time creating new rhythms to rehearse and memorize.

**It should be noted that if you can't mentally recall a rhythm, you should go back to the music and clap it again.*

Advanced Stage

2 Weeks; 15 Minutes Per Day

For the beginning and intermediate level, you were allowed to repeat the exercise on any sound that came natural to you since I didn't specify a timbre to use. For the advanced exercise, your goal is to recreate the sound of various instruments. Start with your own instrument (if you play one), then choose a non-pitched percussion instrument (drum) you like. Once you have done this, you can choose any instruments that interest you. It's not necessary to own these instruments. But you should listen to solo recordings so that you can become familiar with the instrument timbre.

Memorization is no longer the goal, but you can still work to develop your musical memory. At this stage, you should mentally play back as much of the rhythm as you remember. Try to hear a different instrument play the exercise each day. If you need to look at the music at the beginning of your routine, that's okay. However, put the music away and rely on your memory to complete the rest of the exercise as soon as possible. If you have trouble with hearing one instrument, then don't attempt to listen to additional instruments until you have succeeded with just one instrument. Add another instrument only when you're confident you can hear the first instrument clearly. If you don't get past the first instrument this time around, that's perfectly fine.

If you're able to clearly hear an instrument the first week, then progress to the second week and listen to two instruments playing simultaneously. Ideally, you should have one non-pitch-based percussion instrument against a pitch-capable instrument. Try to imagine that the percussion instrument is coming from the left-hand field of your auditory space and the pitched instrument is coming from the right-hand side. Don't attempt to sing a melody, just listen for a single pitched drone on the melodic instrument and play the rhythm. If you have trouble with two instruments at once, try to imagine one instrument holding a drone and bring in the rhythmic instrument once you feel that drone is solid.

This exercise might feel strange at first. If you keep at it and attempt to increase the clarity of each instrument, you will be well on your path to developing a strong inner ear. When you're not working on the exercises during your composing hour, you should be listening to solo works with the instrument you're currently trying to hear. This will help you learn the sound of the instrument, which will make it easier for you to recreate the sound in your mind. If you can, locate a score and follow along with the performance while listening to the instrument. This is a great way to start becoming acquainted with the various capabilities of each instrument.

Once you master your first two instruments playing simultaneously, additional instruments will become easier to hear. It's very similar to the concept of mastering a foreign language. The first language is usually the hardest to learn, but language assimilation gets easier if you try to learn a second and third language. Don't worry too much about how fast you're progressing, just do as well as you can and improve at your leisure.

Advanced Exercise

Week 1

1. During the first week, pick one instrument a day to mentally recall in your mind. Mentally play back as much of the rhythm exercise as you could memorize from the beginning and intermediate stages.
2. Try to make the instrument as realistic as possible.
3. Mentally listen for the duration of your time slot.

The suggested progression is to start with a non-pitched percussion instrument, move to piano, then strings, brass, and woodwinds. This is five instrument groups, which gives you one instrument from each group for each day of the week.

Week 2

During the second week, try to combine the sound of a percussion instrument with one other instrument on the same rhythm. If you're having trouble with this, try the alternate exercise.

1. Aim to hear two instruments distinctly.
   a. Place each instrument in its own registral space (a concept from *The Elements of Music Composition* text) so that it sounds like each instrument is played in its own distinct register.
   b. Don't sing a melody, just mentally hear two pitches playing the rhythm from Exercise 1.1.
2. If you are able to listen to multiple instruments playing the same rhythm simultaneously, the next step is to choose two different rhythms to play at the same time with different instruments. Perhaps you will start by listening to Rhythm

1 and Rhythm 2 from Exercise 1.1 simultaneously. Once you have mastered two rhythms at once, you can try to hear three rhythms at once and then four. Look at the score if necessary, memorization is the goal but not the purpose of this exercise.

Alternate Week 2 (Exercise Modification)

1. Pick an instrument that is easy for you to hear mentally and hold a single drone pitch.
2. Try to imagine a second instrument, or the same one, playing a simple quarter note rhythm above that single drone.
3. If you succeed in hearing two instruments, hold the drone on one instrument and play the exercise on the other.
4. Move on to the standard Week 2 exercise when you've accomplished this.

Exercise Tips

If you're having trouble hearing more than one rhythm, input two rhythms into a notation program or play them on a polyphonic instrument, such as a keyboard. Try to mentally recall what you're hearing after playing the combined rhythm. When you feel comfortable with two rhythms, add the third rhythm, and finally add the fourth. Once you get used to hearing the rhythms, remove the external instrument or notation program.

Using a notation program to hear each rhythm played simultaneously is a good way to get started. However, in the end, don't rely on sampled sounds as the source for your instrument. Sampled sounds can be manipulated to sound somewhat realistic, but you need to know what the instrument actually sounds like in a real-life performance. Even if you want to write sampled music, you still need to develop your ear to recognize the sound of each instrument. This will make it easier for you to create a realistic production of your composition. Listen to several recordings of an instrument to become familiar with the characteristic sound. If you're playing all four rhythms in a music notation program simultaneously, you can remove one rhythm at a time and then mentally play the removed rhythm in your own mind. Continue this until you can hear everything internally.

Don't get discouraged. Even if you have to use an external instrument or notation program, keep working to improve your ear. Eventually, the clarity of the instruments in your mind will improve. For the beginning exercise, don't worry about using a specific instrument, the goal is to simply hear the rhythm internally on whatever instrument comes most naturally to you. If you're like most people, you will likely hear your own voice or the sound of your hands clapping the rhythm.

One way to make the instrument sound clearer in your mind is to change the dynamics. Start softly, then by the fourth measure belt out the rhythm as loud as you can in your mind. Finally, bring the volume down over the last few measures. The simple act of increasing and decreasing the volume can make these instrument timbres come alive for you.

When replaying the rhythms, try to see the score in your mind to improve your ability to memorize and recall music. This is actually a good advanced technique for learning how to write music solely in your mind and then notate it once it's ready. Get away from the time-wasting practice of pecking out notes on the piano, or worse, throwing notes at a notation program to see what sounds good.

First, no matter how good your samples are, if you're using a notation program to compose, you're likely not thinking about the music and how it develops on the most basic level.

Second, notation programs often lack overtones and can't completely replicate live instruments.

If you're having trouble clapping the rhythms, visit UreMusic.com and check the Resources section for some good music notation programs. Some are free and some are paid. Notate the rhythms in the program of your choice and listen to the program play the rhythms back for you. Start by imitating what you hear while following the music. Then, attempt to mentally recall the score and the rhythm during your sessions.

Summary

The rhythm exercises are just the tip of the iceberg. You're on a path toward becoming a better composer if you simply show up each day to attempt the exercises. All it takes is five days a week to become better. If you missed more than half of your days, you should repeat the month. It takes consistent effort every day to create real changes to your technique.

To close off this technique, I'm going to end with a quote by Carl Maria von Weber:

"The most difficult problem of all is to unite voice and instruments so they blend in the rhythmic motion of a piece and the instruments support and enhance the voice in its emotional expression, for voices and instruments are by their very nature opposed to each other."

While this quote refers to the difficulty of getting vocalists and instrumentalists to play together with the same tempo and expressiveness, it also seems to be a good quote for this technique.

There are two ways to approach this technique:

1. Approach it as an exercise that needs to be completed without regard for musicality or the idiomatic tendencies of the particular instruments you choose in the advanced exercise.
2. Use your time to try to hear these rhythms as they would be played idiomatically on each instrument. The pianist attacks a sound with the utmost clarity and with precision. The vocalist uses a bit of rubato and eases into many notes. The violinist takes a moment to reach the heart of a pitch, especially when the music is slow.

Each instrument has its own special characteristics that give the instrument its unique sound. If you have already completed your first month of exercises, keep this in mind for exercises moving forward. You are not just trying to hear instrument timbres (colors); you are trying to develop the ability to recreate a concert in your mind. Treat these simple exercises as you might treat the preparation of a performance on your preferred instrument. Take the time to really get to know the way each instrument sounds so that when you reach the point where you are orchestrating, you will have the ability to hear each sound clearly in your mind.

For this exercise only, you can spend two months developing the technique. If you attempt these exercises again, see if you can get greater clarity and hear the individual instruments as they actually sound. Or, you can push forward and attempt to improve upon your ability by moving on to the next technique.

Ear Training No. 1

Mentally listen to the following exercises during your ear training session. Play these on an instrument or use a recording until you learn the exercise. These drills ***will*** help you develop your ear.

For Ear Training No. 1, sing through Daily Routine No. 1 and the Mirror Exercise No. 1. You should attempt to sing these out loud and hear them internally.

Link to audio: https://mailchi.mp/5f3eab74b0ad/uremusic

Daily Routine No. 1
1
Warmup, Intonation, and Stability
♩ = 102 - 108
9
18
26
2
Interval Isolation - The Perfect Fifth (P5)
41
47
53
59

Interval Isolation - The Perfect Fourth (P4)
3
C Major Scale

C♯ Major Scale
117
126
131
D Major Scale
137
146
151
4
Major Triads
169

Mirror Exercise No. 1

Mirror Exercises

Kevin A. Ure

(1) **The Perfect Fifth (P5)**

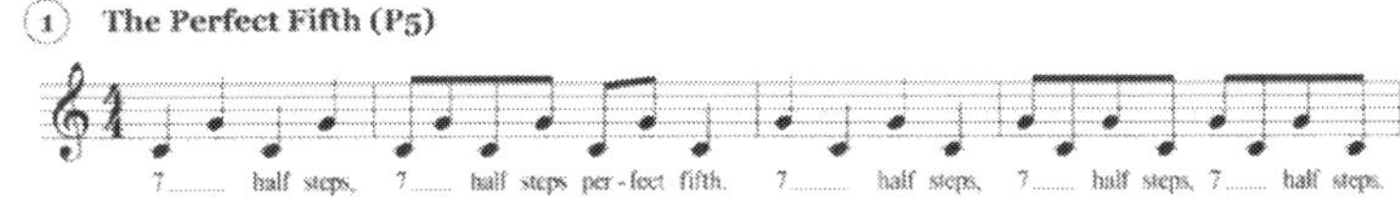

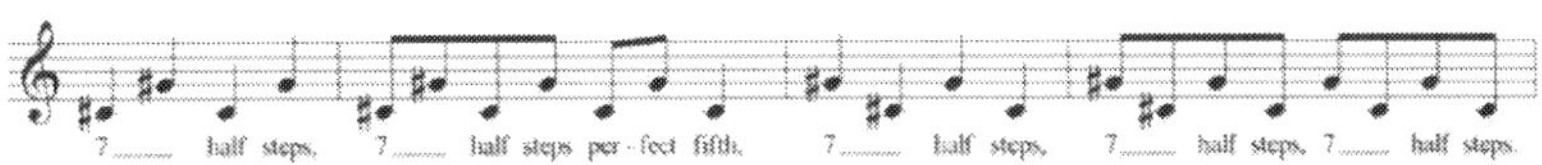

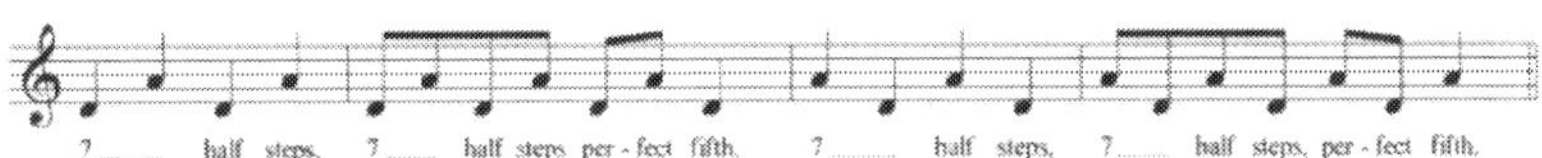

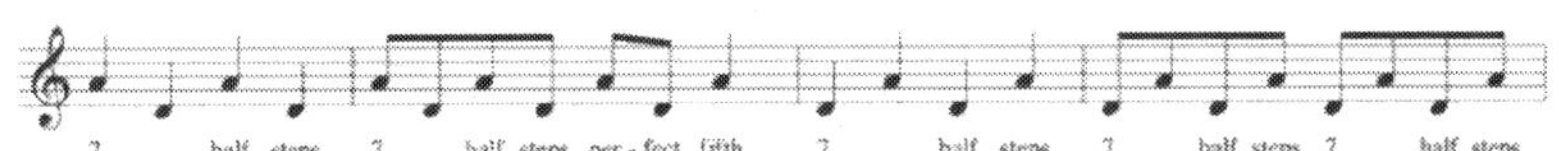

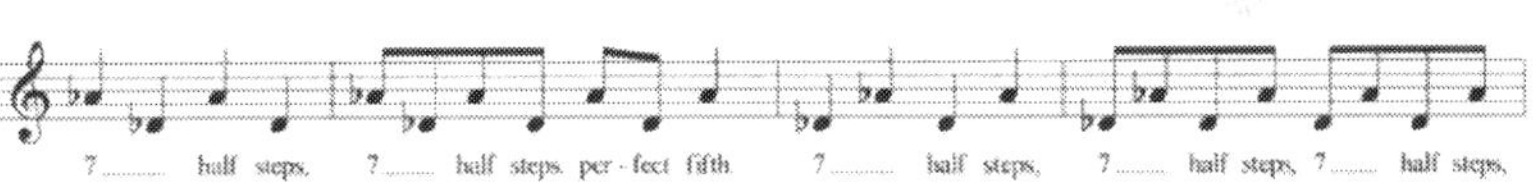

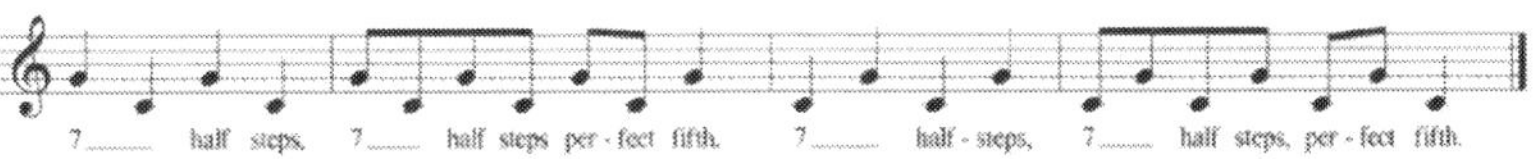

Chapter 5: The Overtone Drone

BUILDING A FOUNDATION

The history of harmony is the history of the development of the human ear, which has gradually assimilated, in their natural order, the successive intervals of the harmonic series.

~ Nadia Boulanger

When I was an undergraduate in the late '90s, I studied under Virko Baley. One day, I was walking to the student union while talking with him. He asked me how my ability to hear multiple voices was doing, and I responded somewhat jokingly that "the voices in my head were getting much better."

When I first started my program, I had already been writing music for several years. However, I'll admit that I was using notation programs, as limited as they were back then, and pecking away at chords on the piano. I hadn't really understood the importance of developing an inner ear. In fact, I didn't even know if it was possible. With the wide range of resources available on the Internet today, I likely could have discovered that it was possible. However, resources for composers were limited at the time, and there were only one or two sources for young composers to communicate in a forum-type setting. YouTube was still a few years off, and Facebook only came onto the scene my first year of graduate school.

Virko was one of the first people to make me realize that plucking away at the piano and using a notation program was a flawed process. I started to realize it was possible to hear an entire musical work in my mind, and this revelation came about partially through the study of other composers. Arnold Schoenberg and

Beethoven were both known for composing music on their walks. Shostakovich was adamantly against composers who "wasted their time" pecking out notes on the piano. Shostakovich suggested composers imagine musical work in their minds before notating it directly in full score.

While I gained confidence that building an inner ear was possible, I wasn't sure how to go about the process. I checked out every sight singing book I could get my hands on from the university library, but I encountered two problems with these books. First, they tended to start mind-numbingly basic and then escalate in difficulty extremely quickly. Second, they never talked about how to develop the ability to mentally hear multiple independent lines. It's one thing to be able to remember a song in all of its detail, it's another entirely to develop the clarity of mind to create music in your head and know exactly what you're hearing.

There are a few things that I've learned about composing music entirely in your head, and I think it's important to share these insights because I know of no single book that attempts to address this issue in a comprehensive manner.

- Unless you are in a state very close to sleep, it is very difficult to compose music completely in your head. When I'm working on a composition, I'll often lie down and access that state just before sleep so that my imagination is stronger. This makes it possible to hear the music with greater clarity. The hardest part is not falling asleep!
- Sometimes you're gifted with a full, concert quality sound, where you might swear that there is an orchestra playing next door. In college, this started to happen to me several times. On more than one occasion, I thought there was a wind symphony or orchestra rehearsing a piece of mine in a nearby room. In most cases, the sound is wispy and not entirely defined. This is

where most composers give up trying, but if you keep trying to envision your composition in your mind, it does gain additional clarity.

- Concentration, at least for myself, is an issue that comes into play when composing. Composing in your mind can take a lot of mental energy at first, which is one reason why this technique builder limits you to 15 minutes per day. If you complete the 15 minutes per day, you won't exhaust your mind. However, you have to exert significant effort to force your brain into realizing composing mentally is a vital skill for your survival. The brain is lazy, and it tends to emphasize the events in your life that scare you or that it *perceives* as putting your life at risk in some way. Whether it's an emotional or physical pain, the brain responds to appropriately stressful events.

I'm relating my own experiences so that you can understand the process I went through and have faith that it can happen for you as well. This training has worked for myself and other students, but you must follow the procedures. Eventually, you will begin to hear entire concerts in your mind with much less effort. I can't guarantee it will ever be effortless, but it's well worth the struggle to develop your talent and let your ability take you as far as possible.

So how do you start building your ear? It all begins with a single drone that you add harmony to over time. I've found that the notes and the sequence of the notes matters in the beginning stages. When I was a student, I tried many different options to develop my ear. The drone method is the technique that ended up giving me the breakthrough I needed to trust that it was possible to compose entirely in my head. It's a very simple exercise, but it produces strong results. This is one exercise that is perfectly fine to practice whenever you're in limbo waiting for something to happen. Maybe it's a line at the motor vehicle department, waiting for your coffee, or just waiting for me to get to the point and give you the assignment. Learn this technique, and you'll never be bored again.

It's worth noting that just because you can practice this technique anywhere, it doesn't mean you don't have to sit down and practice this 15-minute technique as part of your composing hour. Dedicated and focused effort is required for this technique to help you. Daily Routine No. 1 focused on two intervals – the perfect fifth and the perfect fourth. These intervals were chosen for their close proximity to the fundamental note of the overtone series, or as Nadia Boulanger calls it, the harmonic series. A full discussion of the overtone series is available online and in The Musical Core, so I'm not going to repeat that information now. However, if you look at the image below, you can see the overtone series:

Overtones:	Fundamental	1	2	3	4	5	6	7	8	9	10	11	12	13	14	15
Partials:	1	2	3	4	5	6	7	8	9	10	11	12	13	14	15	16

1. The Fundamental pitch is the pitch that you hear, the remaining pitches are overtones that the brain perceives as a part of the initial fundamental. (There is a demonstration of the overtone series on my YouTube channel: https://www.youtube.com/channel/UCUl4QRaP3JAsyBoCnhxTi6Q)
2. The notes in parentheses are out of tune with the natural overtones found in nature.

The overtone series illustrates the relationship between higher overtones and the fundamental tone that we hear. Not all instruments produce overtones. Many electronic instruments are able to play pure sine waves that lack overtones, and some instruments have nearly no overtones at all. Percussion instruments that don't produce specific tones usually don't emit well-defined harmonics or overtones because there isn't a distinct single tone that serves as the fundamental.

Beginning Stage

1 Week; 15 Minutes Per Day

In the beginning stage, your goal is to listen to a single drone that ascends chromatically for a specified length of time. Each note should be held for 20 seconds before moving up to the next note in the series. Use a piano keyboard, your instrument, or an online keyboard to get your starting pitch.

It may be difficult to listen to a single tone for 20 seconds. If you get off track, just redirect your attention and come back to the tone and keep listening. Think of this initial exercise as a meditation, but instead of concentrating on your breathing, concentrate on the tone.

Each measure is numbered to make it easier for you to keep track. Notice that you are arpeggiating through the notes of the overtone series. By keeping this exercise to the opening notes of the overtone series, you are making it easier to mentally envision these pitches. Anecdotally, I find that students develop more quickly when consonant intervals are used in the early stages.

Beginning Exercise

Exercise 2.1 (MM=60)

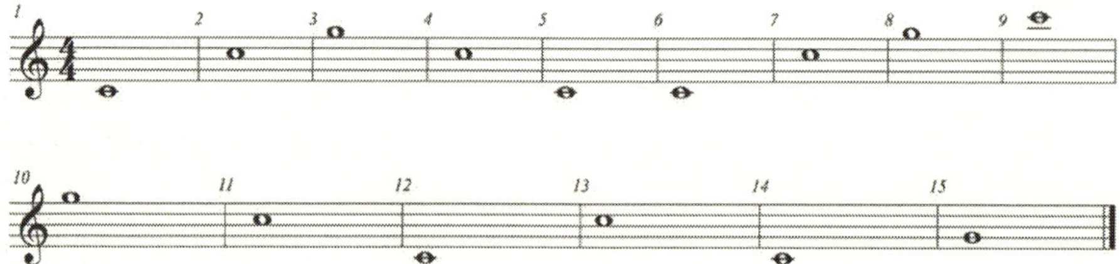

1. Listen mentally to each measure for 20 seconds. This should allow you to complete the first sequence in 5 minutes.
2. Transpose the exercise up a half step and continue to move up chromatically throughout the entire chromatic scale. When transposing, keep the interval qualities the same.
    a. One easy way to do this is to use a key signature. For example, on Day 1, listen to the exercise in C major, C# major, and D Major and move the pitches as needed. C# major will use the notes C#, C#, G# for the first three measures, D major will use D, D, A for the first three measures, and so on.
3. Repeat this exercise for the duration of your 15-minute period. Aim to complete three sequences per day.

    a. **Day 1:** Listen the sequence starting on C, C#, and D.
    b. **Day 2:** Listen to the sequence starting on D#, E, and F.
    c. **Day 3:** Listen to the sequence starting on F#, G, G#.
    d. **Day 4:** Listen to the sequence starting on A, A#, B.

If you have extra days, try listening to the exercise moving from the last measure to the first measure using your favorite keys.

This is not going to be an easy exercise, but it will lay the foundation for future work. It might even be boring, but it's critical that you complete this exercise before moving on to the next stage. Each exercise will get progressively harder, so take the time to let your inner ear develop naturally. If you have to play each pitch on the piano at first, that's okay. But, you should only play the first note of each measure for one beat and then mentally replay it in your mind for the remaining three beats. Aim to get away from the keyboard entirely, except to get your starting pitch.

Intermediate Stage

1 Week; 15 Minutes Per Day

The intermediate stage begins to prime your ear for hearing the intervals that are important for building root position and second inversion chords. Root position chords are chords that are stacked in thirds and have the root of the chord in the bass. First inversion chords have the third in the bass but this exercise doesn't use any first inversion chords because you haven't yet worked on the daily routine that deals with thirds. Second inversion chords have the fifth in the bass. If you are not familiar with inversions yet, just mentally sing through this exercise. When your theory training matches your aural ability, you'll understand why some of the chords are second inversion chords.

The Musical Core teaches you about chords and inversions, but there are also resources online you can use to learn how to spell chords. When you learn about chords and go through this exercise again, you'll have a deeper understanding of how this exercise is constructed.

In the intermediate exercise, you should start by holding a single C drone and gradually add various intervals from the overtone series on top of the drone. You should aim to hear the drone as clearly as possible in relation to the other pitches in the exercise. Again, you should use an instrument to get your pitches if necessary. If you can't hear the interval clearly in your head, then rearticulate the drone every two beats to make it stick out in your mind. You can also try alternating between the top and bottom note until you can hear the two notes simultaneously. Stop after 15 minutes.

Intermediate Exercise

Exercise 2.2 (MM=60)

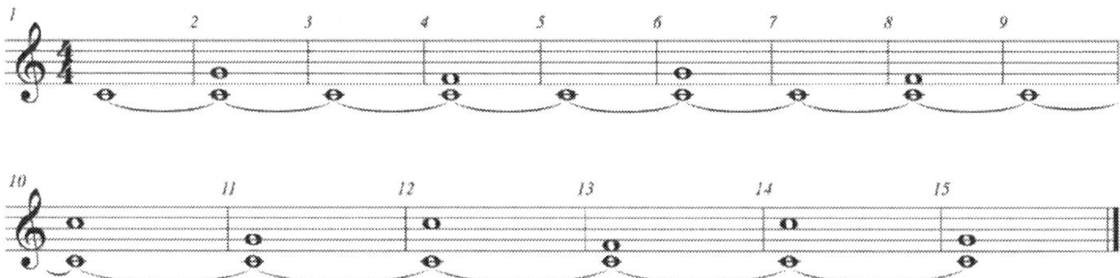

1. Listen to the entire exercise sequence at MM=60. You should get through all 15 measures in about one minute.
2. When it comes time to hear an interval, it's okay if you have to cycle between the top and bottom note at first. The goal is to learn to hear both notes at the same time.*
3. Take the exercise sequence up a half step and continue to move up chromatically throughout the entire chromatic scale.
4. Repeat this exercise for the duration of your 15-minute period. It's fine to take a 15 second break between each sequence. This will allow you to hear the sequence on all 12 chromatic pitches in approximately 15 minutes.

*Cycling refers to mentally playing the top note and then playing the bottom note in the interval. This helps you to gain familiarity and proficiency with the interval since you're "rocking" back and forth between the top and bottom notes. In measure 2 of the example, you might initially hear the G and C as quarter notes that are played melodically (one after another). Once that becomes easier, move to eighth notes, triplets, and sixteenth notes before attempting to hear the intervals harmonically. Playing these on the piano and mentally recalling the interval can also help you to develop the ability to hear harmonically.

Advanced Stage

2 Weeks; 15 Minutes Per Day

In the advanced stage, you are cycling through the lower partials of the overtone series. These notes are the bedrock of most tonally-derived music, so they are some of the most important intervals to be able to identify. Notice how these are all perfect intervals. Remember, perfect intervals fit the overtones series naturally so that they don't have to be adjusted (tempered) to fit our chromatic scales. This is one reason that they are called perfect instead of major since they naturally fit the series. This exercise focuses on the perfect octave, perfect fifth, and perfect fourth.

Advanced Exercise

Exercise 2.3 (MM=60)

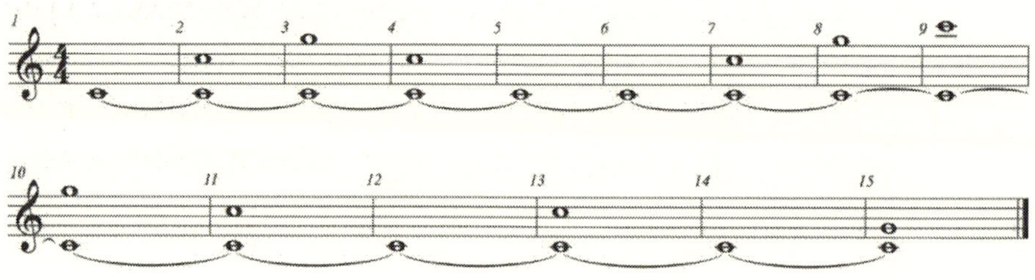

1. Listen to the entire exercise sequence at MM=60.
2. If you need to cycle between the top and bottom interval for the first week, feel free to do so. However, try to avoid cycling between the top and bottom note in the exercise after the first week. The goal is to learn to hear both notes at the same time.
3. Take the exercise up a half step and continue to move up chromatically throughout the entire chromatic scale. Again, you may take a 15 second break after each sequence.
4. Repeat this exercise for the duration of your 15-minute period.

Exercise Tips

It can be difficult to hear more than one tone at first. The following list of suggestions can help you learn to hear two notes at the same time. But remember, don't spend more than 15 minutes per day for the entire exercise.

- Turn the drone into a rhythm to more clearly hear the interval against the sustained note.
- Crescendo and decrescendo one of the intervals to make one note stand out more prominently.
- Hold the drone mentally while playing the other intervals on an external instrument, which could be your own instrument, a piano, or a notation program.
- Rather than keeping a steady tempo, focus on one interval at a time until you can hear the interval.

Even if you can't hear the beginning exercise, it's important you still move forward to the intermediate and advanced exercise on schedule. The result of the exercises in this course is cumulative, and you won't necessarily start to see results until you've gone through a couple months of training.

Stick with the program.

Each new technique isn't necessarily more difficult than the previous technique. Future exercises will help you get better with the previous exercises, even if you haven't yet mastered the earlier techniques.

I'm going to state this again because it's extremely important: *you are not seeking perfection with these exercises.* The goal is to put in an intense and concentrated 15 minutes of effort. Once you have put in the effort, live your life and do something else with your day.

Daily practice will produce substantial results over the new several weeks, months, and year.

Summary

Hearing a drone is how I initially started to develop my ear, and it's worked for many of my students as well. What I have learned is that even if this technique hasn't been mastered, you'll develop more quickly and fully by continuing to the next technique. Many of these techniques are built on processes that train the same basic skills, but in multiple ways. This several pronged approach to developing the ear is what will make this course work for you.

If you only attempt these drills two or three times per week, you're not going to get the results you want. It's very important you commit to at least five days a week to start seeing results from this course. The drone is the first step in developing a sound inner ear that will greatly help you compose more efficiently and fluidly in the future.

Ear Training No. 2

Mentally listen to the following exercises during your ear training session. Play these on an instrument or use a recording until you learn the exercise. These drills ***will*** help you develop your ear.

For Ear Training No. 2, sing through Daily Routine No. 2 and the Mirror Exercise No. 2. You should attempt to sing these out loud and hear them internally.

Link to audio: https://mailchi.mp/5f3eab74b0ad/uremusic

Daily Routine No. 2

Interval Isolation - The Minor Third (m3)
67
73
79
85
91
3
Db Major Scale
106
111

D Major Scale
117
126
131
Eb Major Scale
137
146
151
4
Major Triads
Minor Triads
169

Mirror Exercise No. 2

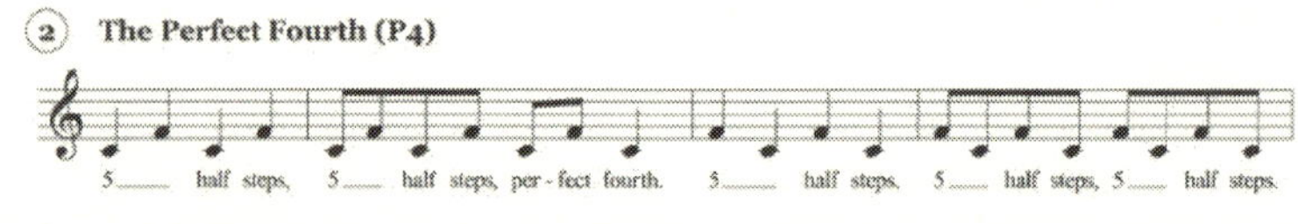

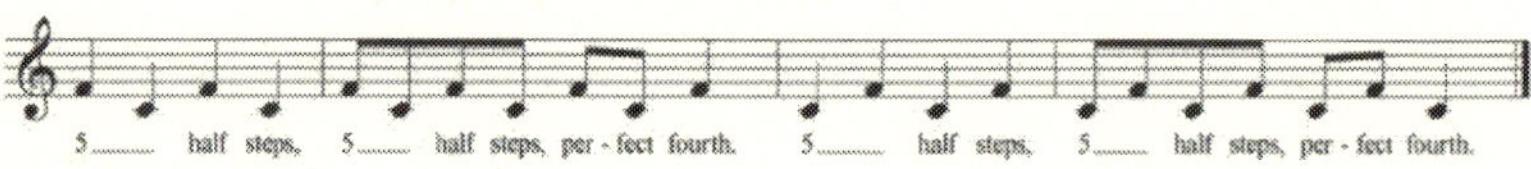

Chapter 6: The Melodic Line

THE PATH TOWARD HARMONY

All musicians practice ear training constantly, whether or not they are cognizant of it. If, when listening to a piece of music, a musician is envisioning how to play it or is trying to play along, that musician is using his or her 'ear' - the understanding and recognition of musical elements - for guidance.

~ Steve Vai

There are plenty of courses designed to develop your ear through the recognition of chords, intervals, scales, and rhythmic dictation. All of these programs can help you develop a better-defined ear provided you practice consistently. However, you must also take the time to improve your ability to imagine your compositions in your own mind. Learning to identify the basic components that make up a musical work is just the start. Singing the melody in a score is one of the first steps toward developing a solid ear. Once you can accurately identify wrong notes in a musical score and sight-read effectively, then it's time to build your inner ear. If you're not yet able to sight-read music, you can still perform the exercises in this chapter. It simply might take you a bit more time to memorize and rehearse the music.

Most ear training courses do not work on the development of an active and imaginative inner musical world; rather, they are focused on getting you to show your technique through singing, and accurately identify intervals, chords, scales, and errors in a score. These are all important skills, but teachers typically don't test the student on the sophistication of the inner ear. Yet, this is perhaps one of the most important skills you can master! You can lose your ability to speak and even lose your hearing, but if you already know how to compose in your mind, nothing will stop you from creating new works.

It's a myth that Beethoven composed deaf. He actually had quite a bit of education, experience, and time before that fate befell him. As he started to lose his hearing, it's reported that he cut the legs off his piano so that he could hear the vibrations more effectively. When Beethoven was realizing he was going deaf, he had to rely more and more on his inner ear. Few would deny that his final works are among his best compositions. He may have closed his lifetime with a severely deficient physical ear, but his inner world and ability to compose music entirely in his mind only became more enriching.

The more accurately you can manipulate ideas in your head, the more efficient you will become at presenting your musical ideas to your waiting public. As with all skills, developing your inner ear will take time, but with continued practice, you can free yourself from the need for computers and musical instruments to hear your music in the external world. Once you get a taste for what it is like to compose music entirely in your head, you'll never want to go back to the computer or piano again. Composing internally is much more rewarding, and your *hardware and software* continues to update free of charge if you put some effort into your composition technique.

This text focuses on giving you the basic structure necessary to develop your inner ear. The good thing about improving your inner ear is that it doesn't require the ability to recognize and identify intervals. Learning the skills of interval recognition, music dictation, and chord identification are important, but these are separate skills that complement your ability to hear music in your mind.

Hearing music in your mind is a distinct skill that benefits you by increasing your ability to accurately hear and notate music, but possessing a good ear is not required to hear music in your mind's ear. If you continue to practice the Daily Routines and the Mirror Exercises, you'll begin to notice that intervals in nature start to pop out at you. Developing the ear is not complicated, but it does take persistence and consistent effort.

Beginning Stage

1 Week; 15 Minutes Per Day

The melody in Exercise 3.1 is designed to be performed as a round. If you had four singers, you could assign each singer a number and the singer would begin at the appropriate time. In this way, melody 1, 2, 3, and 4 create a four-part harmony when all of the parts are sung simultaneously.

If you're not familiar with the concept of a round, singers are assigned a number that indicates the point in the music where they should begin singing from the beginning of the piece. So, group 1 begins the piece at the beginning while the remaining singers stay silent. Then, once the first group reaches point 2, the second group of singers begins singing from the beginning. At this point, harmony is usually created. When group 1 makes it to point 3, they begin singing at the beginning of the piece. Now, 3-part harmony is created. Rounds can consist of 2, 3, or more parts, which can end up resulting in complex melodies.

Beginning Exercise

Day 1: Learn to sing and mentally recall measures 1-8.
Day 2: Learn to sing and mentally recall measures 9-16.
Day 3: Learn to sing and mentally recall measures 17-24.
Day 4: Learn to sing and mentally recall measures 25-32.
Day 5: Attempt to memorize measures 1-32.

Intermediate Stage

1 Week; 15 Minutes Per Day

In the intermediate stage, you will begin to combine multiple melodic lines so that you can begin to hear harmony. This will be a very simple exercise because it's difficult to accomplish. Most musicians will not be able to complete this exercise the first time through, but it's important to spend only one week on this stage and then move on to the advanced stage.

Intermediate Exercise

Day 1: Play the group 2 melody starting in measure 9 on an external instrument. Mentally play the group 1 melody in your mind's ear.
Day 2: Play the group 3 melody starting in measure 17 on an external instrument. Mentally play the group 1 melody in your mind's ear.
Day 3: Play the group 4 melody starting in measure 25 on an external instrument. Mentally play the group 1 melody in your mind's ear.
Day 4: Mentally play the group 1 and group 2 melody simultaneously. Use an external instrument to play the group 3 melody.
Day 5: Mentally play the group 1 and group 3 melody simultaneously. Use an external instrument to play the group 4 melody.

It's not necessary to use the appropriate rhythm and you may play the melody out of time. You may also wish to use a notation program to play the instrumental melodies. It's recommended that you notate Exercise 3.1 by hand for reference.

Advanced Stage

2 Weeks; 15 Minutes Per Day

The advanced stage is very difficult at this point, but don't worry if you're not able to complete this exercise. This course uses a one step forward and two steps back process so that you can continue throughout the entire course. In the next chapter, you will have an easier exercise to complete.

Advanced Exercise

1. Attempt to mentally play back group 1 and group 2 while playing group 3 on an external instrument simultaneously. Move on to Step 2 only when you can complete this process successfully. If you can't do this, don't get discouraged. Work for 15 minutes and then put this exercise aside for the day.
2. Mentally play back group 1, 2, and 3 simultaneously while playing one of these groups that you're having difficult with hearing on an external instrument. Move on to Step 3 when you can complete this process. Go back to Step 1 if you can't complete this step after 3 days.
3. Mentally play back group 1, 2, and 3 while simultaneously playing group 4 on an external instrument. Move on to Step 4 when you can complete this process. Go back to Step 2 if you can't complete this step after 3 days.
4. Mentally play back all of the groups, while playing the melody you are having the most trouble hearing on an external instrument. Move on to Step 5 when you can complete this process. Go back to Step 3 if you can't complete this step after 3 days.
5. Mentally play back the entire round. Go back to Step 4 if you can't complete this after 3 days.

Exercise Tips

This is a challenging exercise, and it will take you some time to learn. It may even require two or three times through this course to develop this ability. Once you are able to successfully complete this exercise, you can find additional canons and rounds in the musical literature to work through to continue developing your skill.

There are several canons as well as duets and solos that you can use to develop your ear. One highly recommended book is "Music for Sight Singing" by Robert Ottman and Nancy Rogers. It's an expensive but classic textbook with plenty of rhythms and melodic examples that many universities around the country use for teaching sight-singing. While I think learning to sing melodies by rote is limited for developing the ability to sight-sing, the Ottman book is great for learning to develop your inner ear.

Don't get discouraged if you're having trouble. Remember, you are only spending 15 minutes of your life per day on these exercises. Eventually, you will develop your ear, but you have to be consistent and persistent. There are no quick fixes to developing your ear and you should expect to spend several years refining your ability to hear music. In the meantime, complete your daily composing hour, write original music, and chip away at your technique incrementally and steadily.

Summary

This exercise can be done with any number of musical examples, and you can even create your own canons. The point is to use an external instrument to get the sound of a second melody into your ear. Then, take away the extra instrument and add an additional melodic line. By doing this, you are slowly developing your ability to hear music internally.

Ear Training No. 3

Mentally listen to the following exercises during your ear training session. Play these on an instrument or use a recording until you learn the exercise. These drills ***will*** help you develop your ear.

For Ear Training No. 3, sing through Daily Routine No. 3 and the Mirror Exercise No. 3 and 4. You should attempt to sing these out loud and hear them internally.

Link to audio: https://mailchi.mp/5f3eab74b0ad/uremusic

Daily Routine No. 3

Interval Isolation - The Minor Sixth (m6)
67
73
79
85
91
3
Bb Major Scale
B Major Scale
104
C Major Scale
111

C Natural Minor Scale
118
127
132
C♯ Natural Minor Scale
138
147
152
4
Major Triads
Minor Triads
170

Mirror Exercise No. 3

Mirror Exercise No. 4

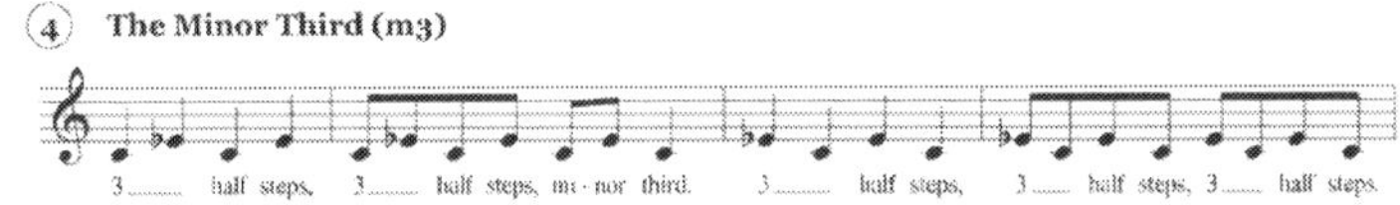

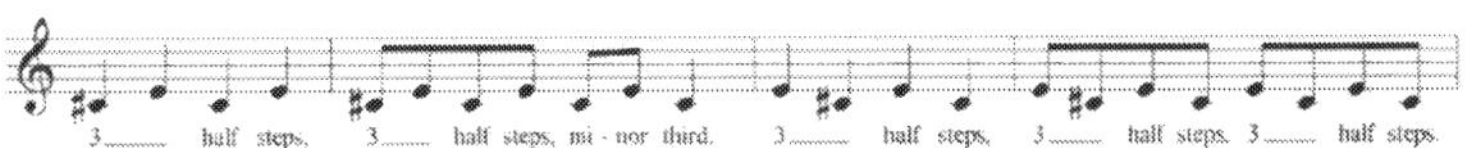

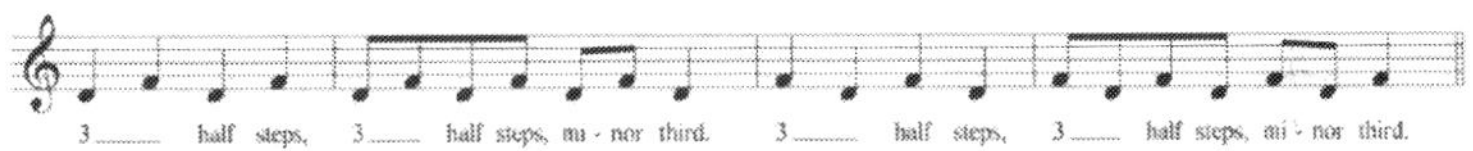

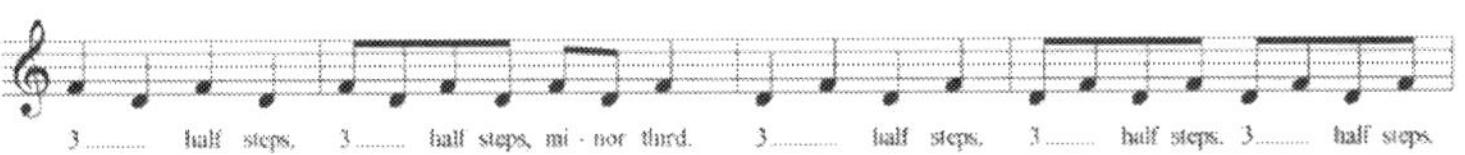

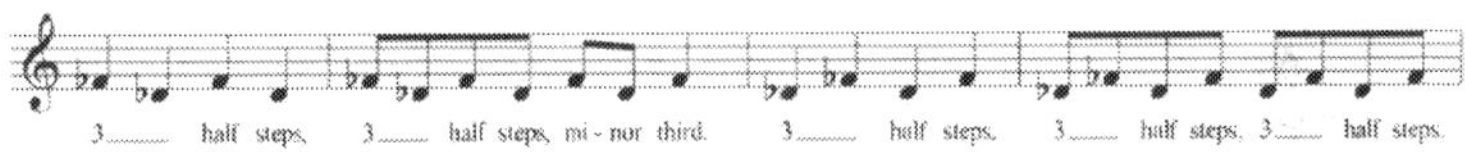

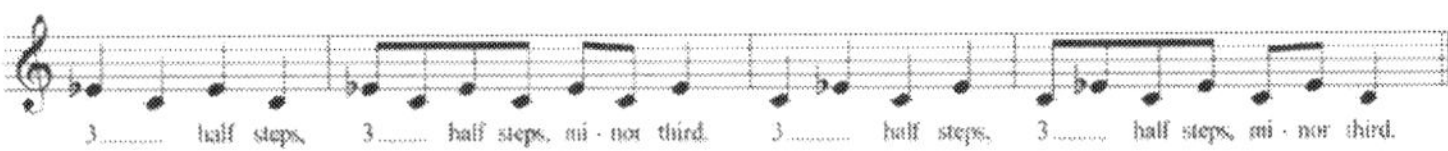

Chapter 7: Harmonic Backdrops

HEARING CHORDS AND TRIADS

Composers are always on the lookout for ways to create new chords. To help you with this process, you will learn three essential techniques you can practice daily to improve your ability to imagine chords. However, it's not enough to hear chords in your mind. You also need to know how to create chord progressions that make sense. Music theory can help you to accomplish this, but you must devote time to studying theory each day. The next volume in this series will introduce you to music theory, but you should begin learning your scales, key signatures, and chords now if you haven't already.

Music theory is an essential tool, and no technique should ever replace it entirely. It's important that you attempt to study music theory weekly so you can continue to advance your skill and knowledge. I also advocate for composers to learn theory so they can use it to develop new methods of composing and not just regurgitate established techniques. If you learn music theory to compose works with chord progressions that work, you'll only end up with music that uses established chords. A composer should strive to push music forward and create new sonorities and not simply be content with a rehashing of what already exists. At the same time, ignoring centuries of musical progress is foolish.

Follow the techniques outlined in this chapter and you'll increase your ability to internalize your music. With daily practice, you'll hear more engaging, interesting and innovative chords based on your own internal environment.

Completing the Exercises

As with the previous chapters, the following techniques should be practiced for 15 minutes a day. Don't worry too much about your progress, just relax, complete the exercise, and then work on your other musical activities.

You'll need a piano for this exercise, but you can use an online piano if you don't have one available to you. You can also download one of the many piano apps available for smartphones. Each stage should be completed on different days and use the recommended progression. You should not complete all of these stages in a single sitting. In the future, you can begin to modify these exercises as you see fit, but for now, please follow the process as outlined. I've used these exercises for years, and I can only promise results when used in the proper order.

Important: Stay on each step for the entire recommended timeframe. Do not move on to the next phase of an exercise until you can complete the previous stage, or I will find you.

Beginning Stage

1 Week; 15 Minutes Per Day

The Interval Stepping Process

This stepping technique is remarkably easy at first, but it is also useful for developing a foundation and the ability to hear intervals and chords. It's based on the premise that before you can hear chords, you need to hear just one note successfully in your mind. Once you can hear a single note, you'll be able to work up to hearing intervals with increasing complexity. Notice we are taking two steps back? This is to build an even stronger foundation so that you see effective progress. I firmly believe in the process of taking one step forward and two steps back.

You should know what an interval is, but if you don't, an interval is a set of any two notes. Intervals can be played harmonically or melodically. If they are played harmonically, you'll hear two notes at the same time. When played melodically, you'll hear the notes played in succession.

These exercises start out simple, so you may be tempted to pass on this exercise with the belief that it's just a waste of your time. However, even the most advanced musician with a perfect ear can benefit from these exercises. If you can already hear music in your mind that is the only reason you should skip this series. Most composers will complete the opening steps without issue, but as the steps become more complex, that's where the real development begins. The first stages prime your mind for more advanced work. At this point, I'm also going to ask you to spend an additional day on these exercises for a total of 6 days.

Beginning Exercise

Day 1: The Single Pitch

1. Close your eyes and play any note on the piano.
2. Let the sound of the note die out completely.
3. Attempt to sing the note once it has died off.
4. While singing the note, play it again on the piano to see if it matches what you're singing.
5. Repeat Steps 1 to 4 with a different note each time. Continue for the remainder of your 15-minute session.

Day 2: Imagining the Pitch

1. Close your eyes and play any single note on the piano.
2. Let the sound of the note die out completely.
3. Listen to the pitch in your mind for 30 seconds. Set a timer.
4. Play the pitch on the piano to verify you have the right pitch.
5. Continue to hold the pitch in your mind and get gradually louder and softer. Make it so loud that you can't hear any of your thoughts and then make it so soft you can barely hear the note at all.
6. Repeat Steps 1 to 5 with a different note each time. Continue for the remainder of your 15-minute session.

Day 3: Adding a Note

1. Play any two pitches on the piano at the same time.
2. Listen to both notes and attempt to sing the lower note.
3. Verify that you are singing the correct pitch by playing it by itself on the piano.
4. Play both pitches again and attempt to sing the top note.
5. Verify that you are singing the correct pitch by playing it by itself on the piano.

6. Repeat Steps 1 to 5 with five different intervals. Continue for the remainder of your 15-minute session.

Day 4: Internalizing Intervals

1. Play any two pitches on the piano.
2. Sing the top pitch and check it against the piano.
3. Play only the bottom pitch while attempting to hear the top pitch in your mind. Check the top pitch against the piano.
4. Play only the top pitch while attempting to hear the bottom pitch in your mind. Check the bottom pitch against the piano.
5. Complete steps 1 to 4 with five different intervals. Continue for the remainder of your 15-minute session.

Day 5: Creating Your Intervals

1. Without a piano, hum any pitch and then listen to the same pitch in your mind.
2. While you keep the pitch going in your mind, imagine a simple rhythm playing along with your single pitch. The rhythm could be a series of quarter notes; it need not be complicated.
3. Add a second pitch on top of the first pitch. Listen to both pitches while you continually repeat the rhythm.
4. Complete Steps 1 to 3 for the remainder of your 15-minute session.

Day 6: Run Through the Process

Run through all five days consecutively. Set a timer for three minutes per stage. Complete the entire series with no rest in-between. This exercise is a technique you can practice daily to improve your ability to compose internally.

Intermediate Stage

1 Week; 15 Minutes Per Day

The Chord Stepping Process

In the intermediate stage, things get more complicated. If you've skipped to this one because you feel the beginning stage is too simple, please complete the beginning exercise before continuing. The first exercise builds a foundation that will help you significantly improve your success and ability to internalize your music. This technique comprises two stages you should combine with the following warm-up daily since you've already developed the capacity to internalize intervals.

Warm-Up (2 Minutes)

Play any pitch on the piano and casually identify any unique characteristics of that pitch. For example, if you were to play an F-sharp and D-flat on the piano, you should notice the F-sharp is more vibrant and twangier in sound. The E-flat is softer and feels more relaxed. This is not the power of suggestion or your piano making this happen. Listen closely, and you'll find each note has its own unique characteristics and those characteristics don't change between instruments.

Don't assign set characteristics, just listen each day and see if you find that individual notes take on specific characteristics. Some people have been able to develop a form of perfect pitch using this process, but it requires significant practice. This is an exercise you can come back to later in the day, but only spend two minutes initially.

Intermediate Exercise

The intermediate exercise will develop your ability to hear chords internally, and it begins with a warm-up each day. The warm-up is an important drill that may help you to develop perfect/absolute pitch over time. I've found this one technique to be the most effective method along with the daily routines for helping students to learn to recognize specific pitches. This exercise uses a combination of singing and mental playback to develop musicianship skills and internal recall.

Day 1-3: Cycling Chord Members

1. Start with the warm-up for 2 minutes.
2. Play any three notes on the piano simultaneously and attempt to cycle through each note in your mind. Don't play each note individually on the piano.
3. Sing the bottom note and then play it on the piano to make sure you sang the correct note. Do the same for the middle and top note.
4. Complete Step 2 and 3 for the remainder of your 15-minute session.

Day 4-6: Extending the Chord

1. Start with the warm-up for 2 minutes.
2. Play any three notes on the piano and attempt to sing each note from the lowest to the highest note. As always, you should also do this in your mind.
3. Add a fourth note and sing from the lowest to the highest note.
4. Add a fifth note and sing from the lowest to the highest note.
5. Repeat Steps 2 through 4 for the remainder of your 15-minute session using randomly selected notes.

Advanced Stage

2 Weeks; 15 Minutes Per Day

Circle of Fifths Rotation

This is a much more complicated task. In this exercise, you'll sing the notes following the circle of fifths with the goal of ending on the correct note. This one may require some work at first to get the initial sequence down. Eventually, since you are mentally playing through this exercise, you will be able to hear this exercise with ease.

Advanced Exercise

The advanced exercise will use two exercises the first week. The first exercise focuses on the Perfect Fifth and Fourth enharmonically speaking. The second exercise will focus on developing your ability to hear chords internally.

Exercise 5.1

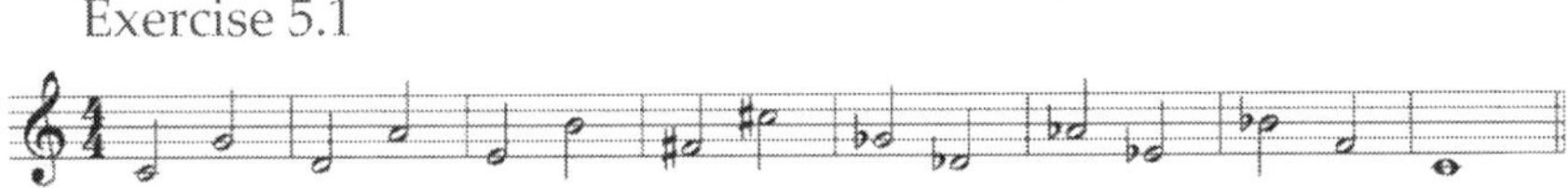

Exercise 5.2

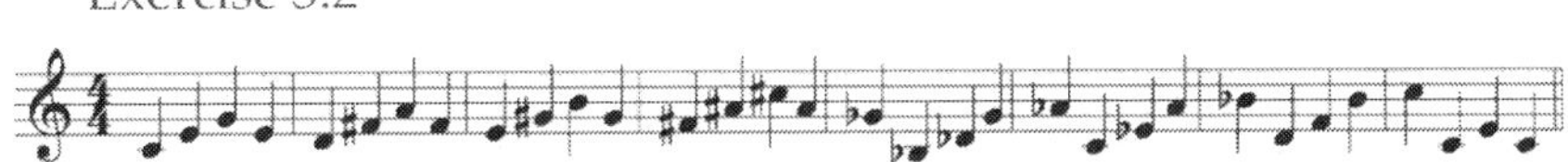

Week 1

Day 1: Playing the Circle of Fifths

Sing Exercise 5.1 while playing along with the piano. Then raise the pitch of the entire sequence a half-step and complete it again.

Day 2: Imagine the Circle of Fifths

Play the first note and then sing Exercise 5.1 without playing the piano. Play the last note when you're finished to make sure you sang the entire exercise correctly.

Day 3: Singing and Rehearsal

Sing Exercise 5.2 while playing along with the piano. Repeat this sequence several times for the remainder of your 15-minute period. Use different tempos to gain better familiarity with the exercise.

Day 4: Leaving the Piano

Play the first note and then sing Exercise 5.2 without playing the piano. Play the last note when you're finished to make sure you sang the entire exercise correctly.

Day 5: Transpose the Circle

Transpose Exercise 5.2 up a half-step and sing without the piano. Play as many keys as possible during your 15-minute practice session.

Day 6: Mental Recall

Play Exercise 5.2 on the piano while mentally recalling the entire exercise.

Week 2

Day 1: Adding a Note I

1. Play any single note on the piano and internalize it in your mind.
2. Sing Exercise 5.1 while keeping the single note playing in your mind.

Day 2: Adding a Note II

1. Play any single note on the piano and internalize it in your mind.
2. Sing Exercise 5.2 while keeping the single note playing in your mind.

Day 3: Adding Intervals I

1. Play any two notes on the piano and internalize them in your mind.
2. Sing Exercise 5.1 while keeping the two notes playing in your mind.

Day 4: Adding Intervals II

1. Play any two notes on the piano and internalize them in your mind.
2. Sing Exercise 5.2 while keeping the two notes playing in your mind.

Day 5: Adding Chords I

1. Play any three notes on the piano and internalize them in your mind.
2. Sing Exercise 5.1 while holding the three pitches in your mind.

Day 6: Adding Chords I

1. Play any three notes on the piano and internalize them in your mind.
2. Sing Exercise 5.2 while holding the three pitches in your mind.

Exercise Tips

When you sing these exercises go slowly, and make sure you're matching the pitch. There are tuners available on the market that will show you what pitch you're playing and how sharp or flat you are. Use these tuners to help you stay on pitch if you're having any trouble. Many of the tuners are free and available for download on your smartphone.

Summary

The aim of this month was to help you start the process of beginning to hear chords internally. Throughout this course, we have been slowly developing your ability to hear music internally. This exercise serves as one of the most difficult parts of the course. If you need to spend two months on this chapter, this is one of the few times where I will recommend you go ahead and take another month to practice. Just don't spend more than two months.

Ear Training No. 4

Mentally listen to the following exercises during your ear training session. Play these on an instrument or use a recording until you learn the exercise. These drills ***will*** help you develop your ear.

For Ear Training No. 4, sing through Daily Routine No. 4 and the Mirror Exercise No. 5 and 6. You should attempt to sing these out loud and hear them internally.

Link to audio: https://mailchi.mp/5f3eab74b0ad/uremusic

Daily Routine No. 4

Interval Isolation - The Minor Seventh (m7)
67
73
79
85
91
3
B Major Scale
D Major Scale
104
C♯ Major Scale
111

D Natural Minor Scale
118
127
132
Eb Natural Minor Scale
138
147
152
4
Dominant Seventh Chords (Mm7)
Minor Seventh Chords (m7)
170

Mirror Exercise No. 5

(5) **The Major Sixth (M6)**

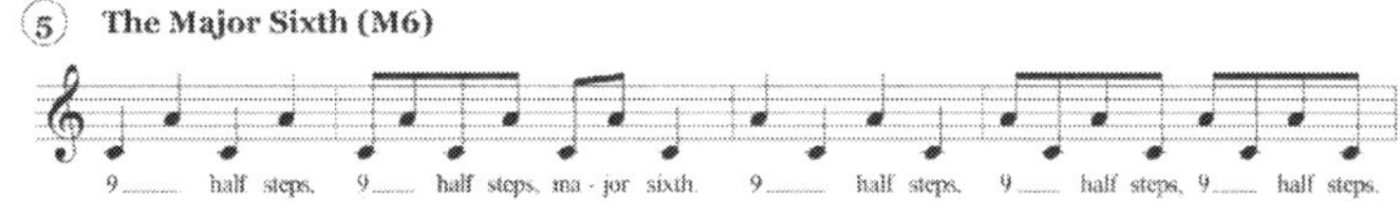

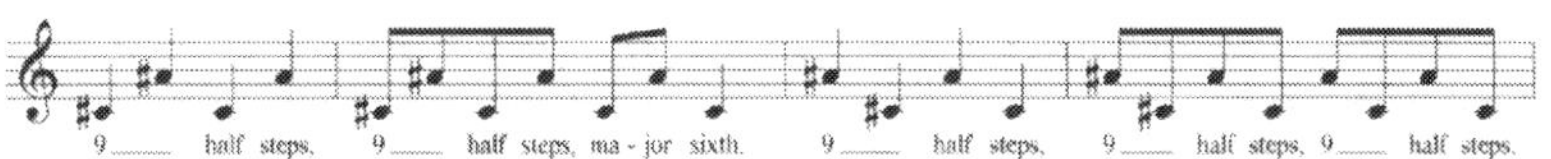

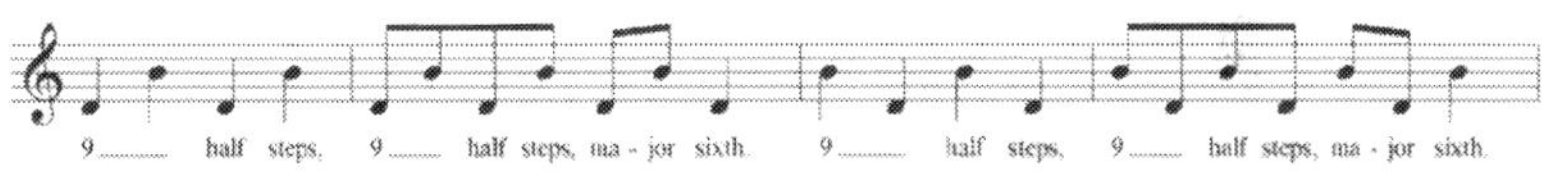

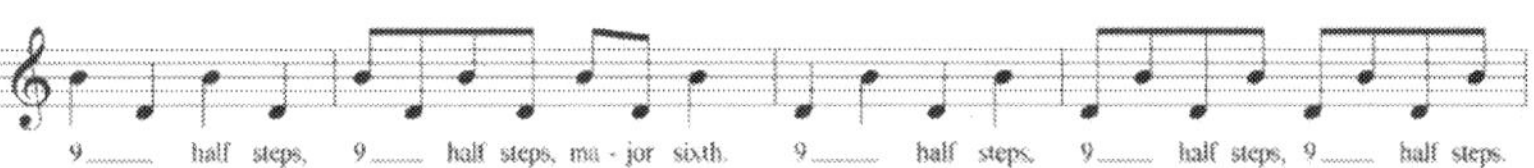

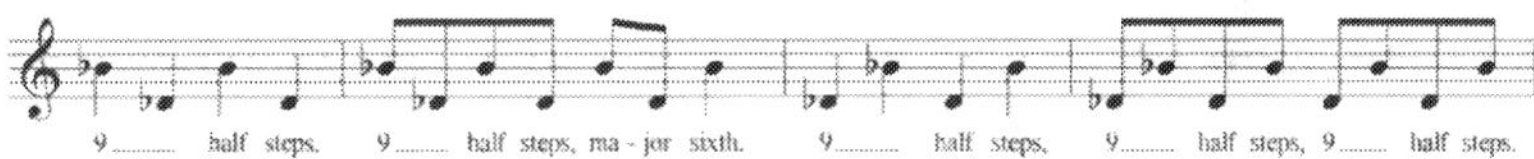

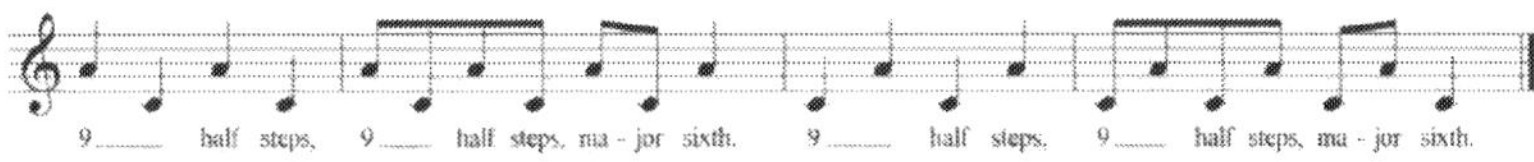

Mirror Exercise No. 6

Part II: Counterpoint

The study of counterpoint is a concept that is first addressed in *The Elements of Music Composition* text. Learning all of the intricacies of counterpoint requires study with a private instructor or a complete course in counterpoint. For the purposes of developing your technique, we will be using counterpoint exercises to develop your ability to hear two-part independent melodic lines. Once you study counterpoint privately, you can begin to create your own two-part, three-part, and four-part counterpoints to continue to develop your ear.

Whenever you attempt to create a counterpoint exercise, it's very important that you attempt to play both the counterpoint and the cantus firmus on the piano. The cantus firmus is the fixed line that cannot be changed by the composer. The counterpoint is the part that the composer writes. For our purposes, you can identify the cantus firmus since it is labeled with "C.F." in the score. If the cantus firmus was not labeled, you could identify it by the last two pitches that utilize modal degrees two and one. So, in the key of C, the last two notes will be D and C in the cantus firmus.

To stretch your ear further, I have created several examples in all of the usable modes from Sixteenth Century Counterpoint. The six modes we will be using are Ionian (C), Dorian (D), Phrygian (E), Lydian (F), Mixolydian (G), and Aeolian (A). These are not the only modes that are used in counterpoint, and you can learn more about the additional modes if you take a complete course in counterpoint.

For this section, we will do away with the beginning, intermediate, and advanced exercises. Simply progress through these exercises at your own pace. Work on each species for one month, and only move on to the next exercise when you can clearly hear both voices in your mind or when you have spent one month on a species, whichever option comes first.

Some of the counterpoint solutions are correct, but slightly problematic since the goal is to keep everything in the treble clef for these exercises. This means the counterpoint range will extend up to A5 in some cases, which is the highest note that a counterpoint should contain. However, since this is a pedagogical exercise and not a theoretical exercise, a few concessions have been made in the interest of simplicity.

Aim to complete two exercises per week. Start by hearing the cantus firmus clearly in your mind. Once you can hear the cantus firmus, add the counterpoint line. Go at your own pace. During your first time through, if you only hear one complete counterpoint exercise per species, you are still making progress. Aim to hear two exercises the next time through this exercise and keep increasing your skill. Remember, this course is designed to be used repeatedly. Each time you go through this course, you will gain additional fluency and proficiency in these exercises.

A student who has never trained the ear can expect to see results in approximately one to four years with steady and consistent training. There are no quick fixes.

While it's highly recommended you take counterpoint with a competent instructor or through a university, *The Craft of Music Composition* does provide instruction in counterpoint. However, studying counterpoint on your own poses problems since most students need an instructor to point out any mistakes.

Chapter 8: First Species Counterpoint

NOTE AGAINST NOTE

First species counterpoint occurs when there is a single note against note relationship between the cantus firmus and the counterpoint. Aim to learn the cantus firmus first and then add the top voice.

For our purposes, first species is a good option to start with because there is no dissonance allowed in first species counterpoint. You will only be working with the intervals of a perfect unison, perfect fifth, perfect octave, thirds, and sixths. This limits the kind of harmonies that you will hear, which will make it easier for you to develop your inner ear. It's permissible to repeat a note once, but unisons are not allowed in the middle of the counterpoint. To maintain the sound of the mode, the counterpoint should always begin or end on a perfect fifth or perfect octave when the solution is provided above the cantus firmus. For the purpose of this text, the "rules" don't matter since all of the exercises have been created for you.

You may notice that the Phrygian mode is the only mode that doesn't end with a half step between the final two notes of the counterpoint. This follows the convention of not raising the seventh mode in Phrygian since there is a half-step relationship between the first and second modal degree of the Phrygian mode. The half step between the second modal degree and the first in Phrygian is often referred to as the "descending leading tone."

As a refresher, the leading tone is the seventh scale degree of a major key. In minor, the seventh scale degree is referred to as the subtonic when the natural key is used. Typically, the subtonic gets raised a half step to create a leading tone relationship between the seventh scale degree and the first.

First Species Exercise

1. Sing the cantus firmus aloud. (This is always the lower line in these exercises.)
2. Mentally play back the cantus firmus.
3. Sing the counterpoint (you may need to take it down an octave.)
4. Sing the counterpoint while you mentally play back the cantus firmus. (If you took the counterpoint down an octave, take the cantus firmus down an octave as well.)
5. Attempt to mentally play back the entire counterpoint exercise.
6. Once you can mentally play back the counterpoint exercise, move on to the next example and repeat Steps 1-5.

Ionian

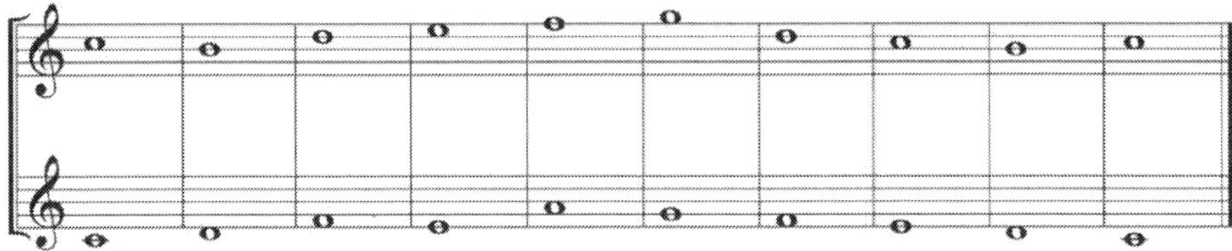

Ionian

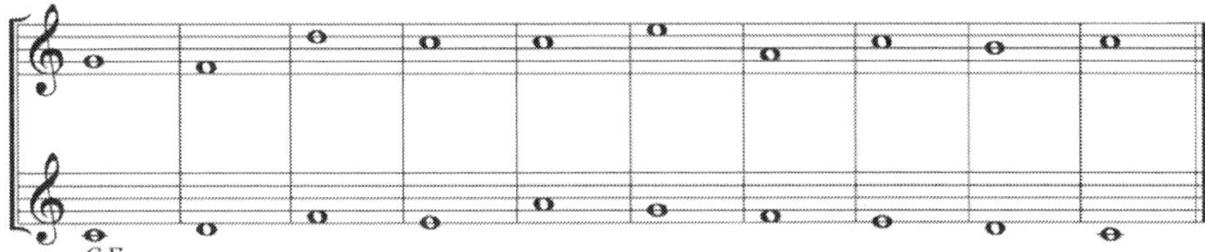

Ionian

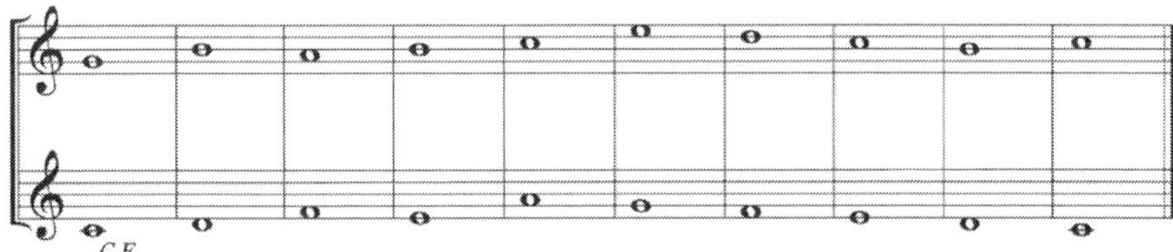

Dorian

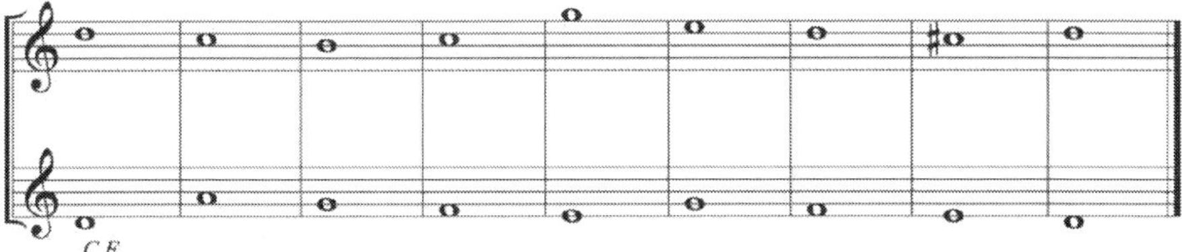

Phrygian

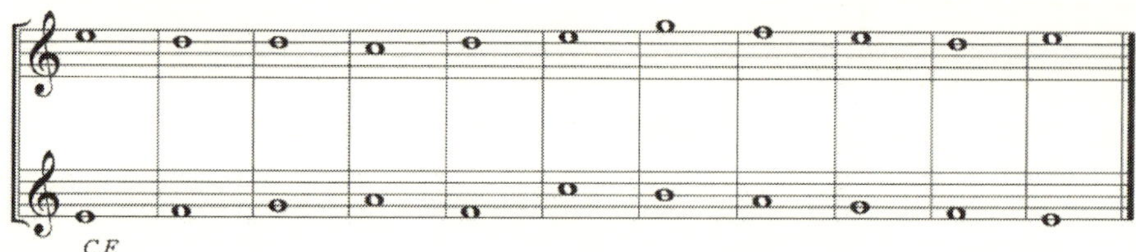

C.F.

Lydian

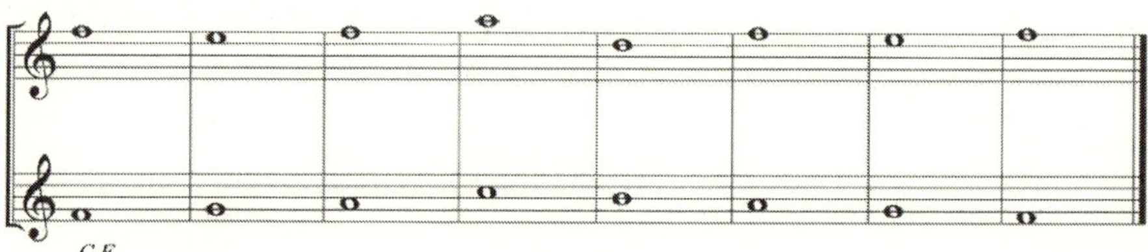

C.F.

Mixolydian

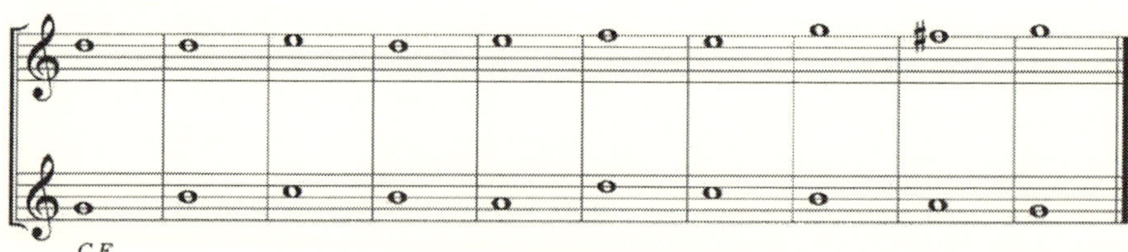

C.F.

Aeolian

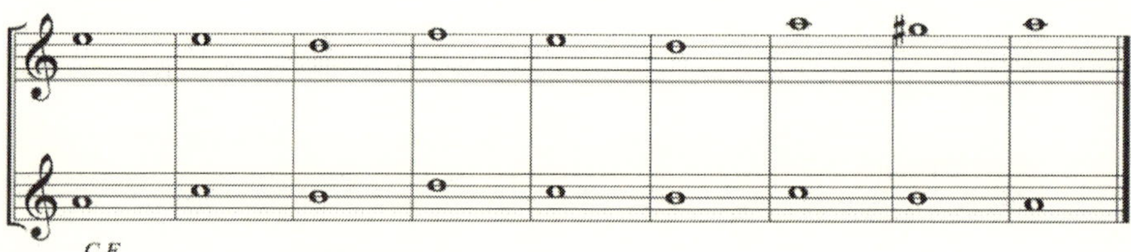

C.F.

Ear Training No. 5

Mentally listen to the following exercises during your ear training session. Play these on an instrument or use a recording until you learn the exercise. These drills ***will*** help you develop your ear.

For Ear Training No. 5, sing through Daily Routine No. 5 and the Mirror Exercise No. 7 and 8. You should attempt to sing these out loud and hear them internally.

Link to audio: https://mailchi.mp/5f3eab74b0ad/uremusic

Daily Routine No. 5
1
Warmup, Intonation, and Stability
= 102 - 108
9
18
26
2
Interval Isolation - The Tritone/Augmented Fourth/Diminished Fifth (TT/A4/d5)
41
47
53
59

Interval Isolation - The Perfect Octave (P8)
67
73
79
85
91
3
C Major Scale
C♯ Major Scale
104
D Major Scale
111

E Natural Minor Scale
118
127
132
F Natural Minor Scale
138
147
152
4
Major Triads
163

172
Minor Triads
180
188
195
Diminished Triads
202
210
P5
5 Dominant Seventh Chords (Mm7)
6 Minor Seventh Chords (m7)

Mirror Exercise No. 7

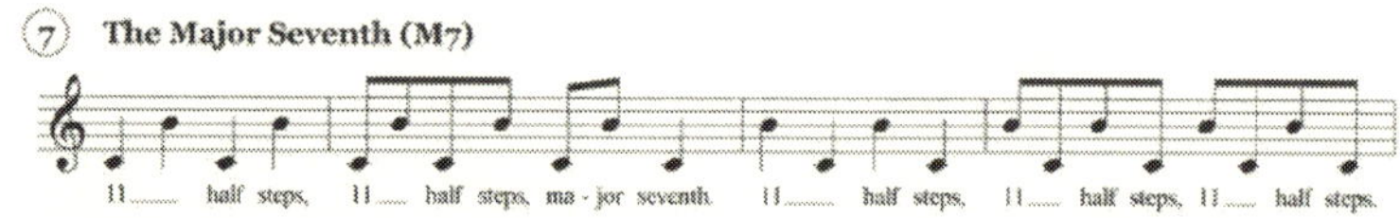

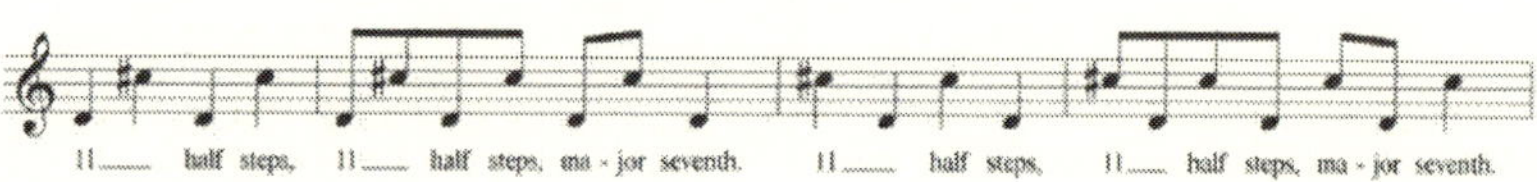

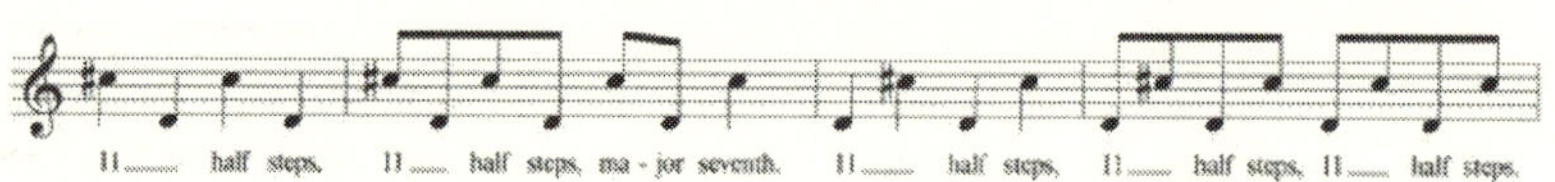

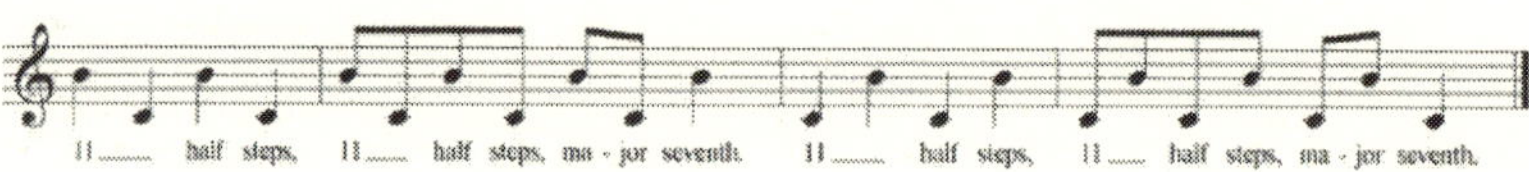

Mirror Exercise No. 8

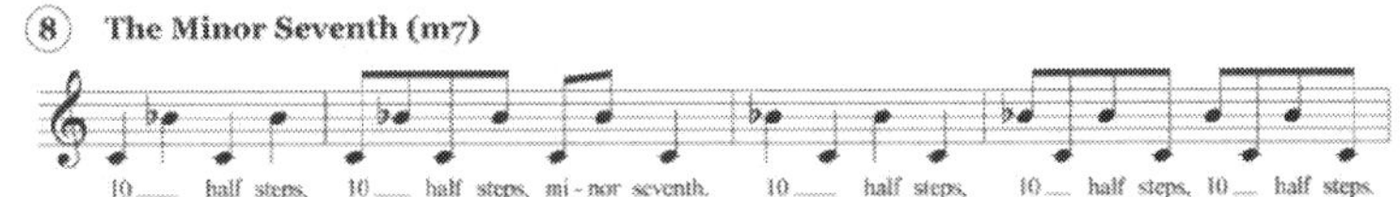

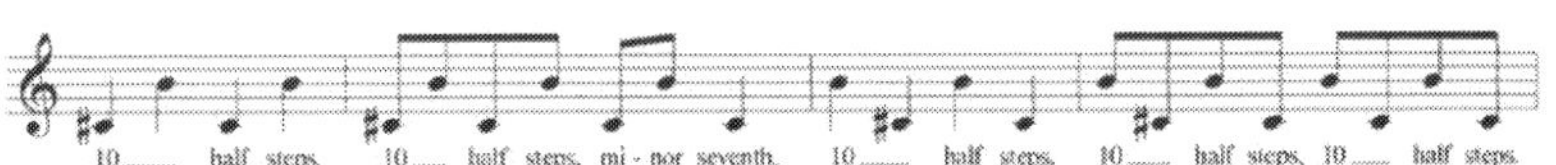

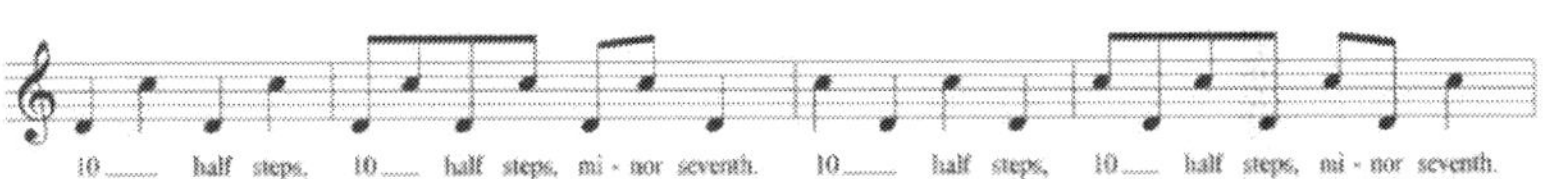

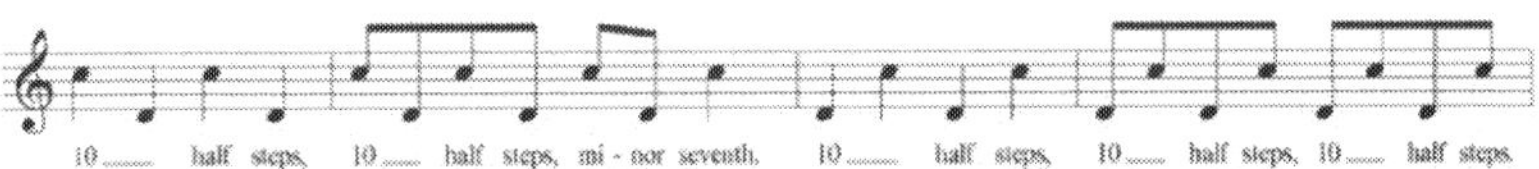

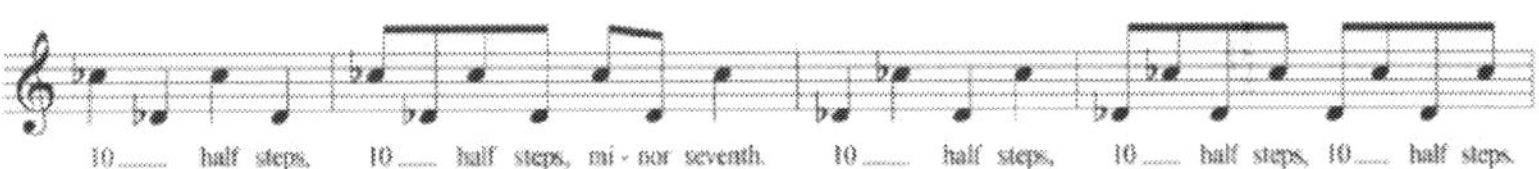

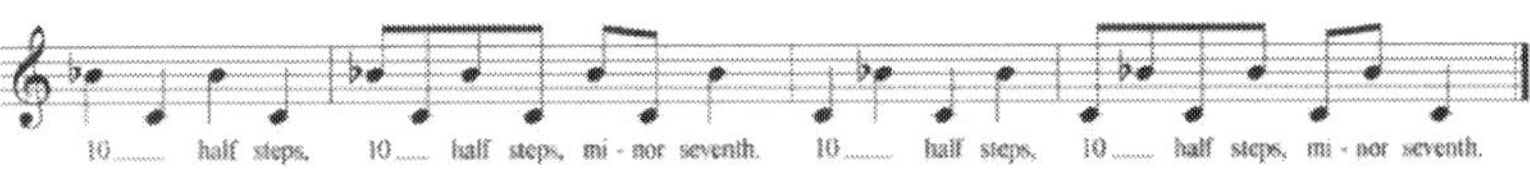

Chapter 9: Second Species Counterpoint

TWO AGAINST ONE

In second species counterpoint, there are two notes for every one note of the cantus firmus. At this point, dissonance is now allowed on the weak beats of the counterpoint solution. The aim of second species is to use dissonances on the weaker beats to propel the piece forward. With first species exercises, the counterpoint tends to sound very stable due to the large number of consonances on the downbeats.

The composer will aim to have a single high point in the cantus firmus and avoid faulty motion, including downbeat to downbeat perfect consonances. Melodic fourths are allowed, but these should not be used harmonically. Some other unique differences from first species includes the ability to begin on a rest, repeated notes are no longer allowed, and unisons are now allowed on the weak beats.

The same cantus firmus will be used for the second species exercises since the goal is to help you develop your ability to hear two independent lines. By using the same cantus firmus, you can spend more time practicing the new exercises.

Second Species Exercise

1. Sing the cantus firmus aloud. (This is always the lower line in these exercises.)
2. Mentally play back the cantus firmus.
3. Sing the counterpoint (you may need to take it down an octave.)
4. Sing the counterpoint while you mentally play back the cantus firmus. (If you took the counterpoint down an octave, take the cantus firmus down an octave as well.)
5. Attempt to mentally play back the entire counterpoint exercise.
6. Once you can mentally play back the counterpoint exercise, move on to the next example and repeat Steps 1-5.

Ionian

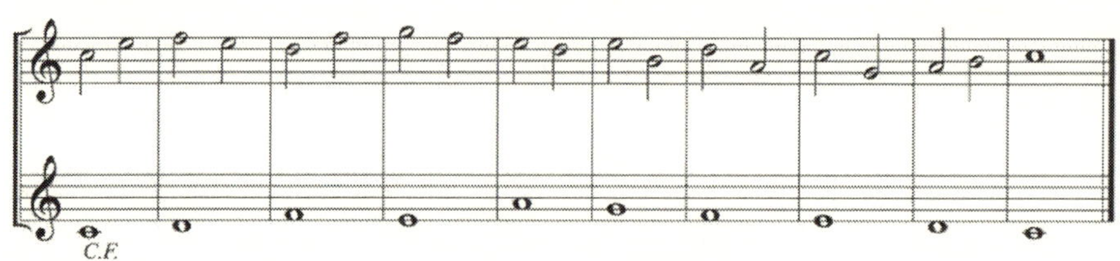

Ionian

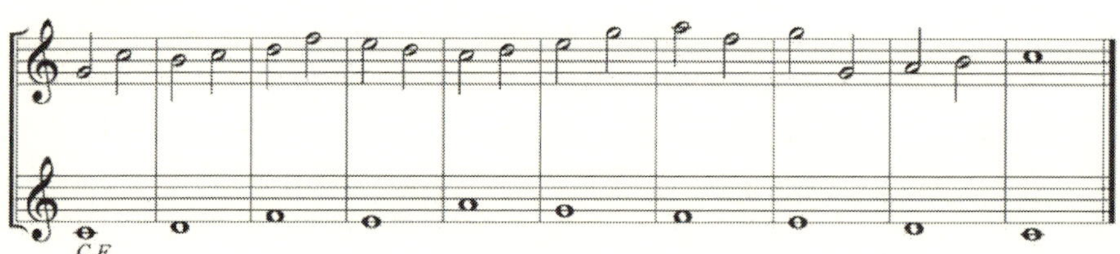

Ionian

Dorian

Phrygian

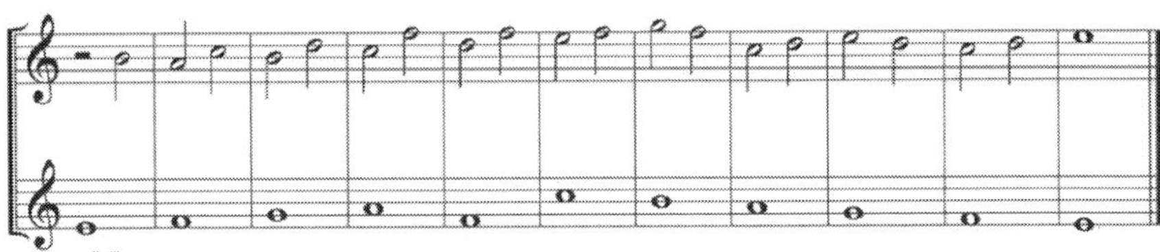

Lydian

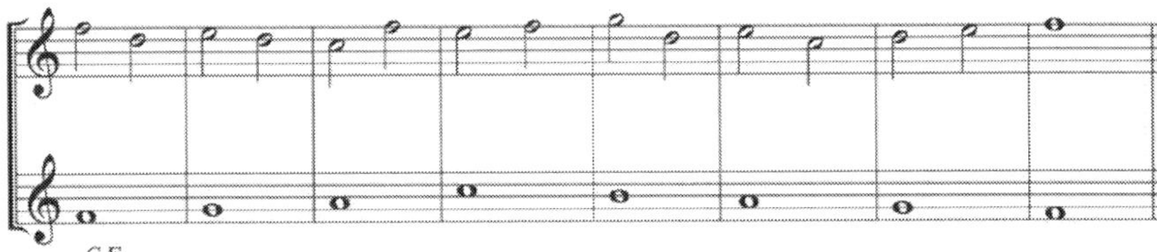

Mixolydian

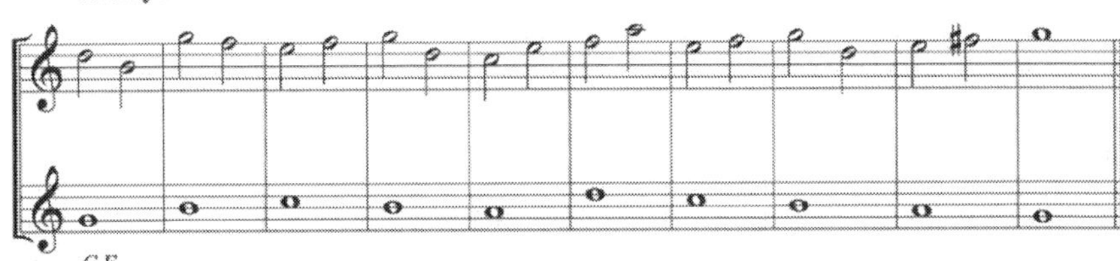

Aeolian

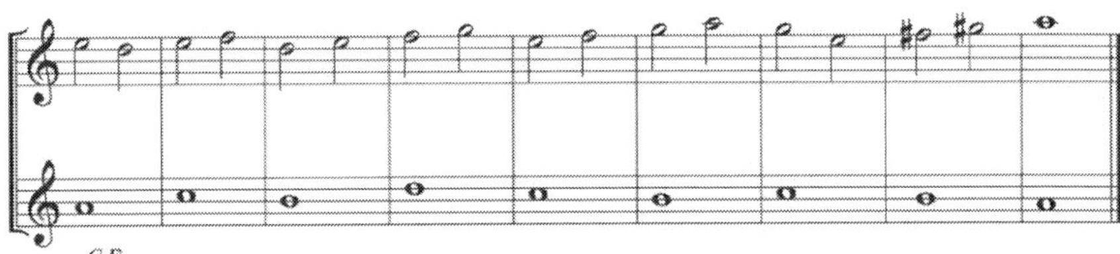

Ear Training No. 6

Mentally listen to the following exercises during your ear training session. Play these on an instrument or use a recording until you learn the exercise. These drills ***will*** help you develop your ear.

For Ear Training No. 6, sing through Daily Routine No. 6 and the Mirror Exercise No. 9 and 10. You should attempt to sing these out loud and hear them internally.

Link to audio: https://mailchi.mp/5f3eab74b0ad/uremusic

Daily Routine No. 6

3 Interval Isolation - The Minor Second (m2)
78
84
90
96
4 C♯ Major Scale
1 2 3 4 5 6 7 1 1 7 6 5 4 3 2 1 1 3 5 3 1 3 5 3 1
F♯ Natural Minor Scale
109
1 2 3 4 5 6 7 1 1 7 6 5 4 3 2 1 1 3 5 3 1 3 5 3 1
G Natural Minor Scale
116
1 2 3 4 5 6 7 1 1 7 6 5 4 3 2 1 1 3 5 3 1 3 5 3 1

C Harmonic Minor Scale
1 2 3 4 5 6 7 1 7 6 5 4 3 2 1
1 2 3 4 5 6 7 1 1 7 6 5 4 3 2 1
1 2 3 4 5 6 7 1 7 6 5 4 3 2 1 1 3 5 3 1 3 5 3 1 3 5 3 1
C♯ Harmonic Minor Scale
1 2 3 4 5 6 7 1 7 6 5 4 3 2 1
1 2 3 4 5 6 7 1 1 7 6 5 4 3 2 1
1 2 3 4 5 6 7 1 7 6 5 4 3 2 1 1 3 5 3 1 3 5 3 1 3 5 3 1
5 Major Triads
Ma - jor triad 4 then 3 half steps. Ma jor triad 4 then 3 half
steps. Ma jor triad 4 then 3 half steps. Ma jor triad

4 then 3 half steps. Ma - jor triads ___ 4 then 3 half steps. Ma - jor triad ___
Minor Triads
Mi - nor triad ___ 3 then 4 half steps. Mi - nor triad ___ 3 then 4 half
steps. Mi - nor triad ___ 3 then 4 half steps. Mi - nor triad ___
3 then 4 half steps. Mi-nor triad ___ 3 then 4 half steps. Mi-nor triad ___
Diminished Triads
6
Dominant Seventh Chords (Mm7)
Minor Seventh Chords (m7)

Mirror Exercise No. 9

9 The Perfect Octave (P8)

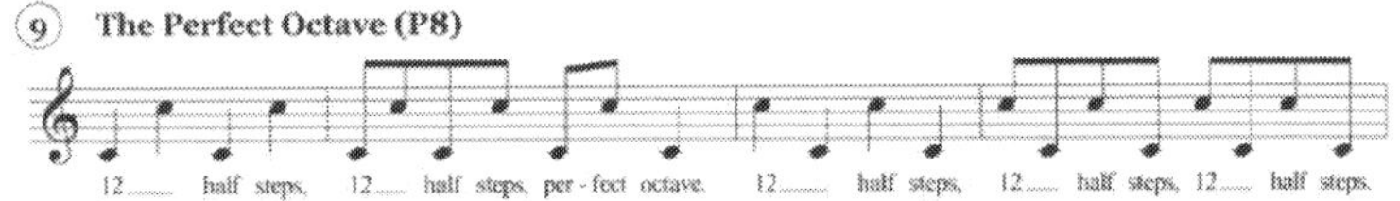

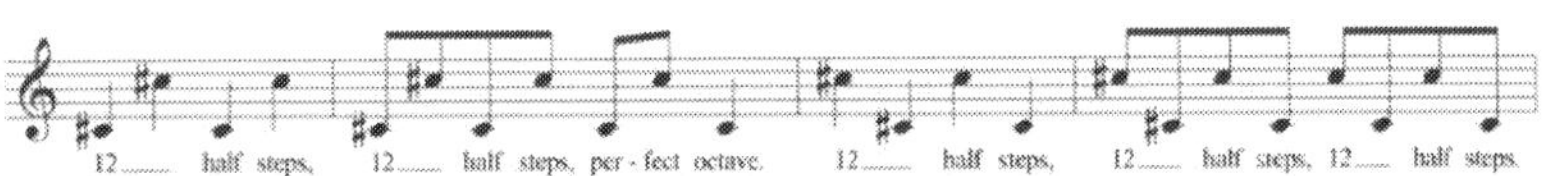

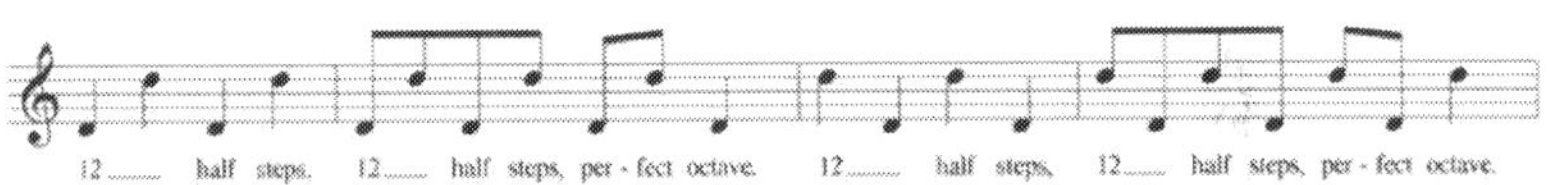

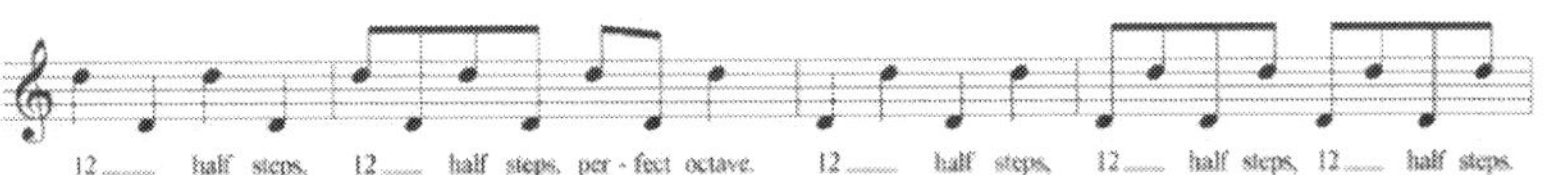

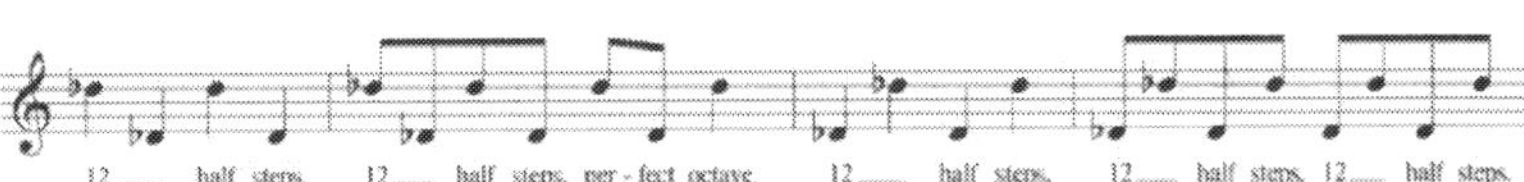

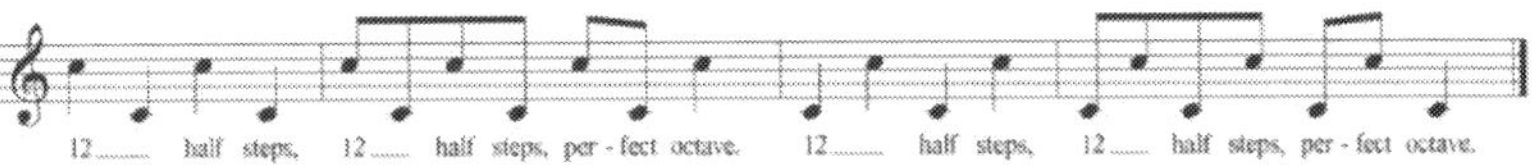

Mirror Exercise No. 10

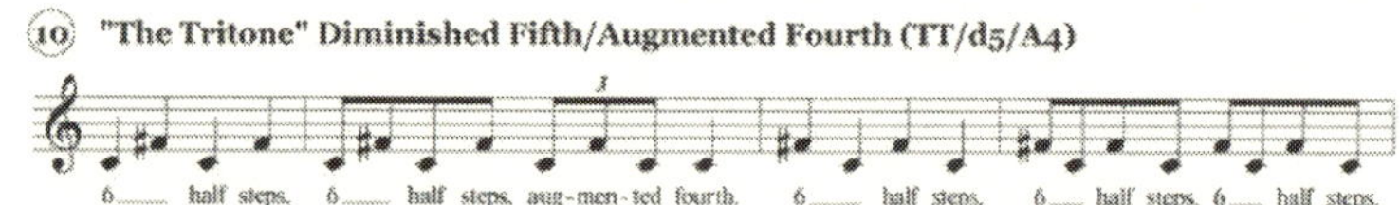

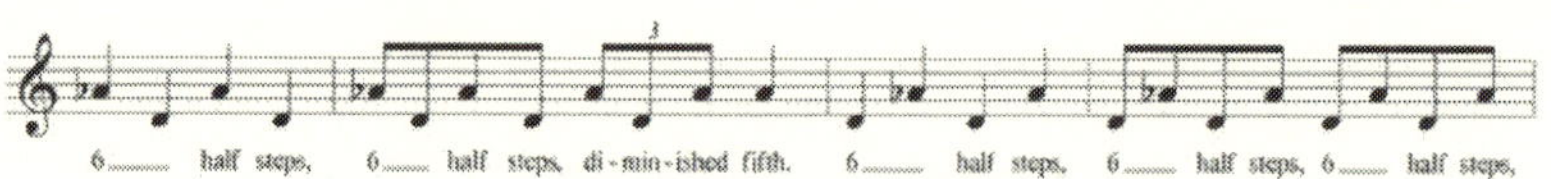

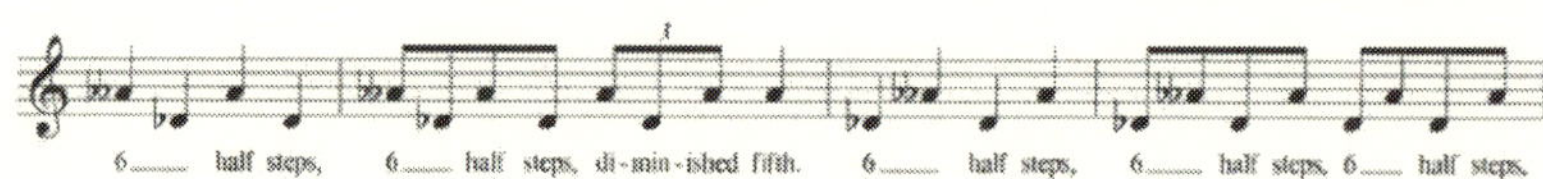

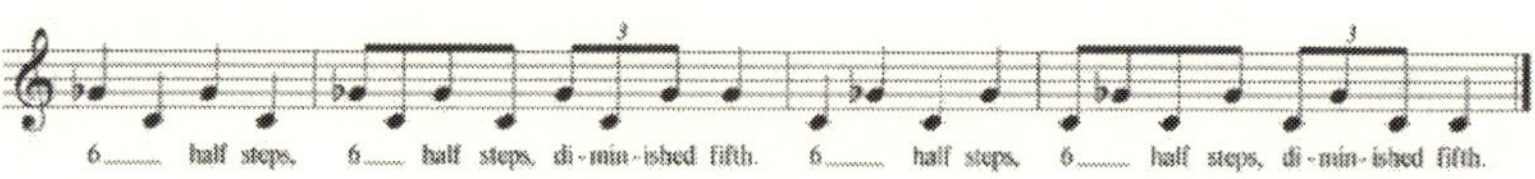

Chapter 10: Third Species Counterpoint

FOUR AGAINST ONE

While there are actually five species of counterpoint, we will end our practice with the third species. For additional exercises, it's recommended you begin studying counterpoint so that you can learn to create your own counterpoint exercises. By learning to create counterpoint exercises on your own, you will be honing your craft and developing your ability to compose more effectively.

Third Species Exercise

1. Sing the cantus firmus aloud. (This is always the lower line in these exercises.)
2. Mentally play back the cantus firmus.
3. Sing the counterpoint (you may need to take it down an octave.)
4. Sing the counterpoint while you mentally play back the cantus firmus. (If you took the counterpoint down an octave, take the cantus firmus down an octave as well.)
5. Attempt to mentally play back the entire counterpoint exercise.
6. Once you can mentally play back the counterpoint exercise, move on to the next example and repeat Steps 1-5.

Ionian

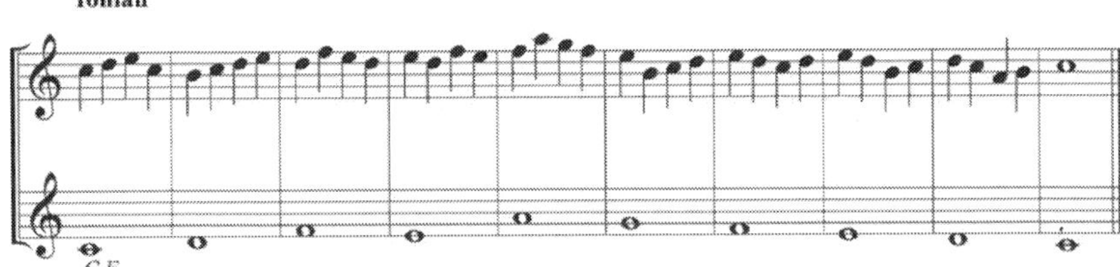

Dorian

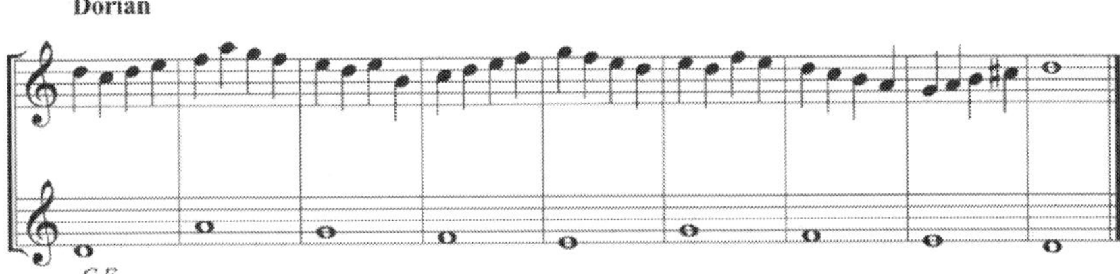

Phrygian

Lydian

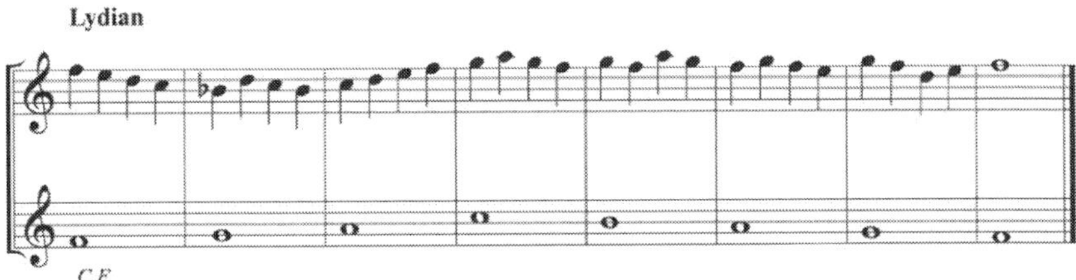

Ear Training No. 7

Mentally listen to the following exercises during your ear training session. Play these on an instrument or use a recording until you learn the exercise. These drills ***will*** help you develop your ear.

For Ear Training No. 7, sing through Daily Routine No. 7 and the Mirror Exercise No. 11 and 12. You should attempt to sing these out loud and hear them internally.

Link to audio: https://mailchi.mp/5f3eab74b0ad/uremusic

Daily Routine No. 7

Daily Routine No. 7

mi nor seventh
Per fect octave per fect octave
Per fect fifth per fect fifth per fect fifth
per fect fifth
per fect fourth per fect fourth per fect fourth per fect fourth
Ma jor third
ma jor third ma jor third ma jor third
Mi nor third mi nor third mi nor third mi nor third
Ma jor sixth ma jor sixth ma jor sixth ma jor sixth
Mi nor sixth mi nor sixth
mi nor sixth mi nor sixth
Aug-men-ted fourth aug-men-ted fourth di-min-ished fifth di-min-ished fifth
3 Major, Natural Minor, and Harmonic Minor Scales
1 2 3 4 5 6 7 1 1 7 6 5 4 3 2 1 1 2 3 4 5 6 7 1 1 7 6 5 4 3 2 1 1 3 5 3 1
1 2 3 4 5 6 7 1 1 7 6 5 4 3 2 1 1 2 3 4 5 6 7 1 1 7 6 5 4 3 2 1 1 3 5 3 1
1 2 3 4 5 6 7 1 1 7 6 5 4 3 2 1 1 2 3 4 5 6 7 1 1 7 6 5 4 3 2 1 1 3 5 3 1

4 C Melodic Minor Scale
5 C♯ Melodic Minor Scale
6 Major Triads (M)
Ma - jor triad
ma - jor mi - nor thirds.
Ma - jor triad
ma - jor mi - nor thirds.
Ma - jor triad

Minor Triads (m)
Mi - nor triad mi - nor ma - jor thirds. Mi - nor triads
mi - nor ma - jor thirds. Mi nor triad
Augmented Triads (A or +)
Aug men ted triad ma - jor ma - jor thirds. Aug men ted triad
ma - jor ma - jor thirds. Aug - men - ted triad
Diminished Triads (d or o)
Di - min - ished triad mi - nor mi - nor thirds. Di min ished triad
mi - nor mi - nor thirds. Di - min - ished triad
7
Major Seventh Chord (M7)
Ma - jor se - venth chord ma - jor tri ad ma - jor seventh. Ma - jor
se venth chord. ma jor tri ad ma jor seventh. Ma jor se venth chord.

Dominant Seventh Chord (Mm7)
221
Do mi nant___ se venth chord ma jor tri ad mi nor seventh. Do - mi - nant___
226
se venth chord ma - jor tri - ad mi - nor seventh. Do - mi - nant___ se venth chord.
Minor Seventh Chord (m7)
231
Mi - nor___ se - venth chord mi - nor tri___ad mi - nor seventh. Mi - nor___
236
se venth chord. mi - nor tri - ad mi - nor seventh. Mi - nor___ se - venth chord.
Half-diminished Seventh Chord (dm7)
241
Half di - min - ished se - venth chord di - min - ished triad mi - nor seventh. Half di - min - ished
246
se venth chord. di - min - ished triad mi - nor seventh. Half di - min - ished se - venth chord.
Fully-diminished Seventh Chord (d7)
251
Fully di - min_ished se - venth chord di - min - ished triad dimin - ished seventh. Fully di - min_ished
256
se venth chord di - min - ished triad dimin - inshed seventh. Fully di - min - ished se - venth chord.

Mirror Exercise No. 11

(11) **The Major Second (M2)**

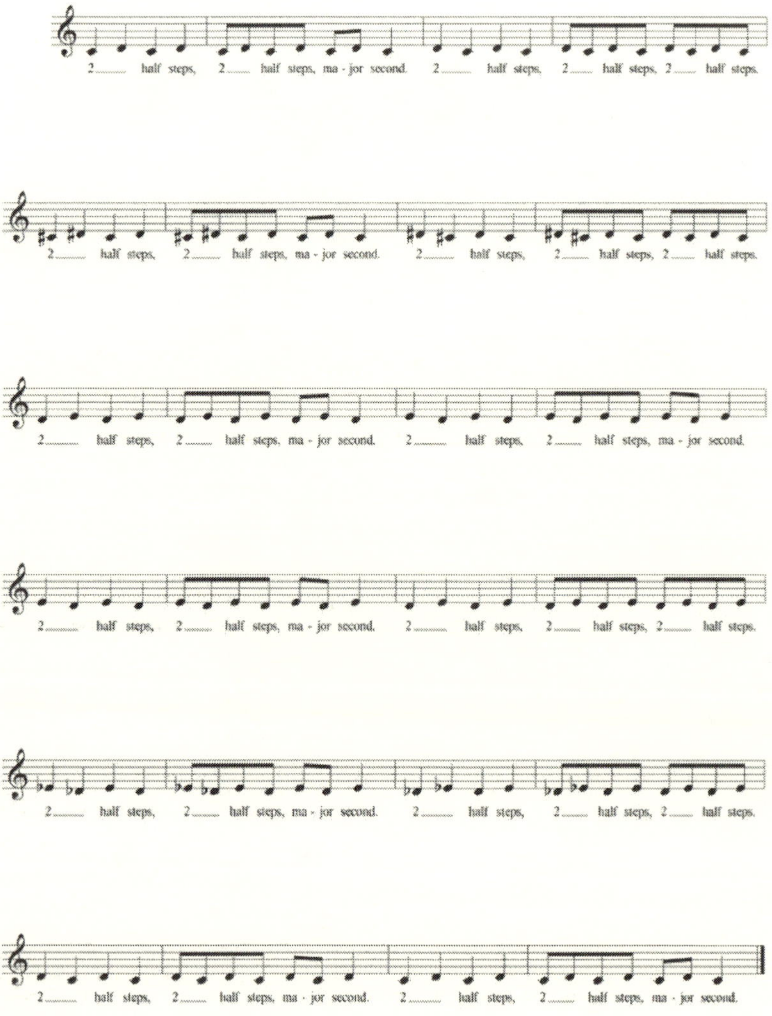

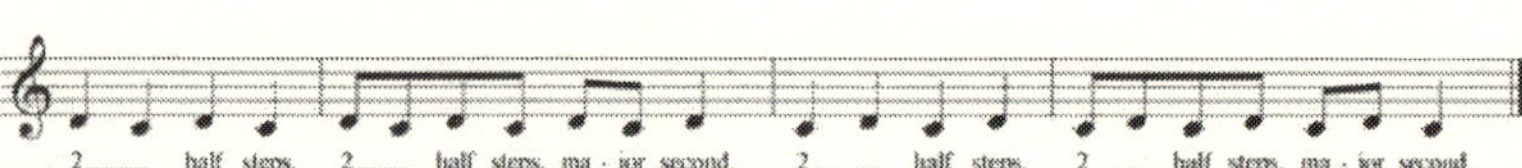

2 half steps, 2 half steps, ma - jor second. 2 half steps, 2 half steps, 2 half steps.
2 half steps, 2 half steps, ma - jor second. 2 half steps, 2 half steps, 2 half steps.
2 half steps, 2 half steps, ma - jor second. 2 half steps, 2 half steps, ma - jor second.
2 half steps, 2 half steps, ma - jor second. 2 half steps, 2 half steps, 2 half steps.
2 half steps, 2 half steps, ma - jor second. 2 half steps, 2 half steps, 2 half steps.
2 half steps, 2 half steps, ma - jor second. 2 half steps, 2 half steps, ma - jor second.

Mirror Exercise No. 12

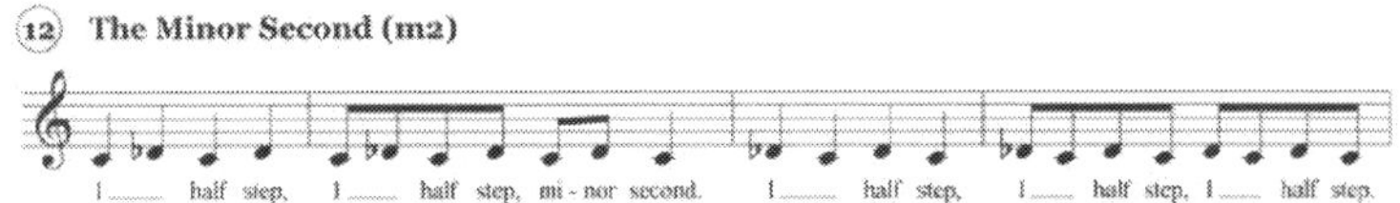

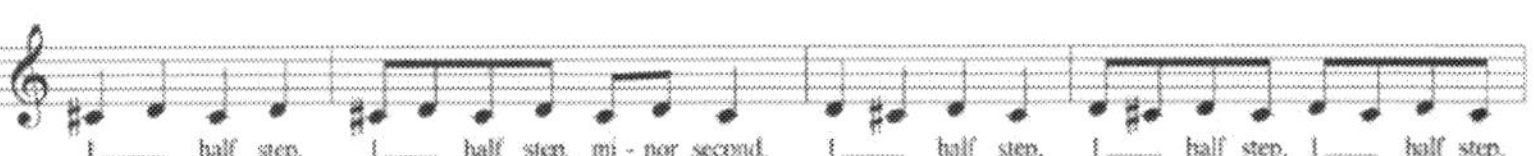

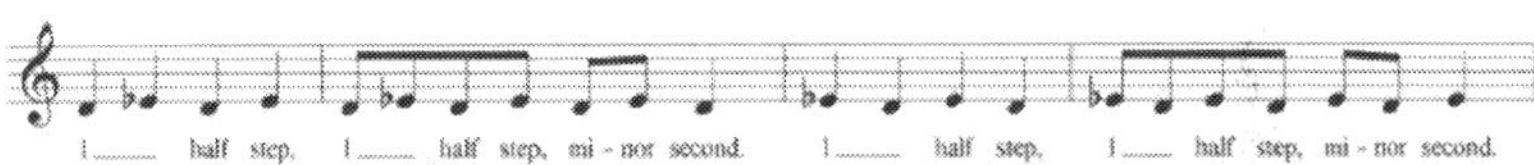

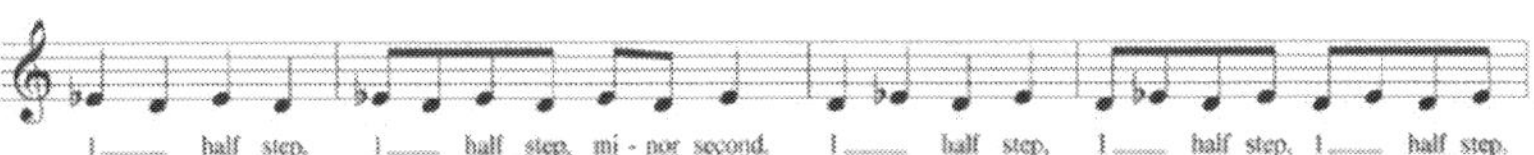

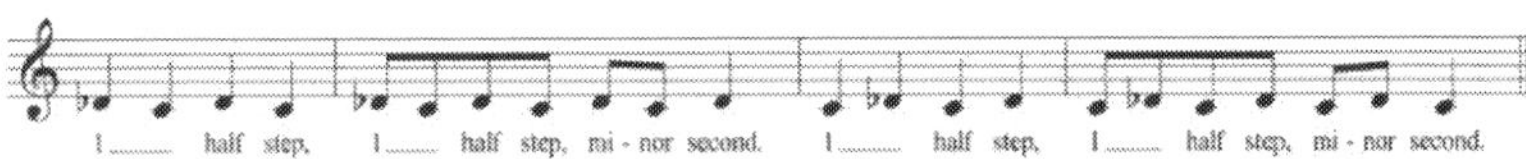

Additional Ear Training Exercises

At this point, you can continue to work on any of the previous ear training exercises. There is also an extended workbook with additional exercises that can be purchased separately (available in 2020). However, you do not need to purchase this workbook. Start by reviewing the ear training exercises that gave you the most difficulty. Then, attempt to create some of your own or continue with the *Music Composition Technique Builder (Workbook).*

This course will continue to challenge your ear with additional exercises. However, the Daily Routines and Mirror Exercises are designed to help you develop fundamental skills that will be useful for several different styles of music. The two components are designed to be completed quickly so that you can hone your skills without spending a significant amount of time each day on ear training. Don't worry about how fast you are developing, just sing through the Daily Routines and Mirror Exercises and you'll find that your ear will naturally develop over time.

Part III: Composing Music Guide

Part III of the Technique Builder is less sequential than the previous parts. This part focuses on providing tips for developing your inner ear and composing music. You'll find many of the techniques in this part of the guide may require you to complete some of the legwork on your own. In this sense, this section serves to function as a series of masterclasses.

The chapters in this part are taken directly from masterclasses that I have provided to my private students. While these exercises can help you to develop your ear, the goal of this section is to get you started on the path toward thinking about music composition and analysis as related subjects. Part III also gives you some valuable tools that you can use to develop your career as a composer.

This part returns to some of the concepts from the first part of the course. However, this time, the concepts are presented in a manner that is designed to help you develop the same basic skills in a less structured and regimented manner. Once you complete Part III, you should start over and complete this text again so that you can continue to develop as a composer and musician.

Unlike the earlier stages, there are no time limits on how long it takes you to complete the exercises in this part. Take your time, and only move on to the next chapter when you can complete each chapter successfully. If this part is difficult for you, then I suggest starting over with Part I again while spending 15 to 30 minutes per day on the chapters in this section. In this way, you'll work on Part I+II and Part III simultaneously.

Remember, the most important thing you can do to develop your ear and internal mind is to keep working at a slow but steady pace. Eventually, you will develop the skills you crave.

Chapter 11: Music Analysis

DEVELOPING THE INNER EAR

All musicians practice ear training constantly, whether or not they are cognizant of it. If, when listening to a piece of music, a musician is envisioning how to play it or is trying to play along, that musician is using his or her 'ear' - the understanding and recognition of musical elements - for guidance.

~ Steve Vai

Preparing the Foundation

There are plenty of courses designed to develop your ear through the recognition of chords, intervals, scales, and rhythmic dictation. All of these programs can help you develop a better-defined ear provided you practice consistently. However, you must also take the time to improve your ability to imagine your compositions in your own mind.

Most ear training courses fail to work on the development of an active and imaginative inner musical world. The more accurately you can manipulate ideas in your head, the more efficient you will become at presenting your musical ideas to your waiting public. As with all skills, developing your inner ear will take time, but with continued practice, you can free yourself from the need for computers and musical instruments to hear your music in the external world.

Musical Analysis

This composition exercise will start with a simple piece to get you started. We will use Mozart's Piano Sonata No. 16, K. 545. This piece is a simple composition with high clarity between the voices. By using a simple piece like this, you can improve your ear gradually before attempting the more complicated task of composing your music in your mind's ear. We are using Mozart because the music is clearly written, which is perfect for our purposes. If you wish, you can choose another piece. If you like this exercise, you can add it to your daily practice routine and continually find new pieces to enjoy.

Download the recording and score for the Mozart piano sonata. (Available on IMSLP.org)

The scores are also available at:
https://mailchi.mp/5f3eab74b0ad/uremusic

Score: Piano Sonata No. 16, K. 545
Recording: Piano Sonata No. 16, K. 545

Preparatory Stage

The first stage of learning to develop your internal ear is to listen to a piece and become familiar with it. Follow the steps provided and take your time to ensure that you have mastered each step before moving on to the next one. There is no reason to rush through this as you are only competing with yourself.

If you find this stage difficult, just stay on the current step until you're able to complete it effortlessly. The brain learns with repetition, so it may just require several weeks, months, or even a year before you can master each step. As you improve, you'll find it will take less time to complete this task with new pieces. Take your time, go at your own pace, and don't rush. Ideally, you should spend a few weeks working on each step.

For this stage, you will follow a simple meditation to prime the brain for more advanced work. Follow the steps to help develop your ability to imagine your music. It's fine to repeat this exercise several times per day.

1. Imagine a single drone (sustained note) in your mind's ear. Close your eyes and let it get louder and softer. Don't change the pitch, just keep a solid tone going. Set a timer for five minutes and try to make the tone louder and clearer as you listen. Complete this step at least five times on five consecutive days before moving on to Step 2. The ideal time to practice this is before taking a nap or going to sleep. You want it to be the last thing you bring your mind's attention to before your brain organizes the information for the day.

2. Set the timer for another five minutes. Start your drone on any pitch and then imagine a percussive sound playing

accents against the drone every few seconds. It doesn't have to be in time. The goal is to create a drone and a second sound within your mind's ear. Do this for at least two consecutive days. Judge for yourself, if you find this step easy, then do it for only two days. Otherwise, continue practicing at this level until you find it effortless.

3. Set your timer for another five minutes. Start your drone and attempt to hear a melody on top of the drone. The melody doesn't have to be difficult or interesting. Practice listening to two separate ideas in your mind's ear.

If this exercise is easy for you, you can move on to the Intermediate stage. Otherwise, continue to complete each step until you can easily complete all three steps. This is a progressive exercise. Once you have mastered each step, you need not return to a previous stage unless you feel your ability languishing.

Intermediate Stage

After completing the preparatory stage, it's time to move on to something more complicated. If you made it through the first stage, you should be proud of your accomplishment. It's not an easy task, and learning to hear your internal melodies can take a long time to develop.

1. Listen to the first movement of the Mozart piece while following along with the score. Listen to the piece at least three times even if you have already played this work before or know it well. Move on to Step 2 only when you can follow along and not get lost during the first movement.

2. Put the audio recording away. Attempt to imagine the sound of the music while reading the score. You're most likely not reading the music at this point. Instead, you are just using the score to help you remember the sound of the music. Move on to Step 3 only when you can read the score and internalize the music with high reliability. Go back to Step 1 as needed until you can read through the entire score while playing it back in your mind.

If you can't read music, think of the score as a map. It's not important to understand what every symbol means, but the visual cues can help you remember the piece. You should begin working on your ability to read music, and *The Musical Core* from Kendall Hunt Publishing Company can help you along this path. When you're unable to read music, it's like you're seeing in black and white and other composers are getting full color. You're missing a huge part of the process.

3. Listen to the audio recording a few more times to refresh your memory. Grab the score and try to hear only the top line while

reading the score. Listen along with the recording while trying to isolate the top line in your head and separate it from the bottom line. Do the same thing with the bottom line after mastering the top line. Move on to Step 4 once you can hear each line.

4. Now that you can hear the top and bottom line, it's time to put both parts together in your own mind and put away the recording. While following the score, attempt to hear both lines playing at the same time. Sit back and enjoy the concert going on in your mind. Complete this exercise daily in a meditative manner and with additional musical works. As you get better, you'll find that the quality of the instruments gets louder and clearer.

Don't worry if you have trouble completing these steps at first. Use a simpler piece and work your way up to this composition. A good option for those who need something a little simpler is Mozart's Minuet in F Major, K.2. Complete this exercise daily for at least 30 days and jump for joy when Mozart finally invades the space between your ears.

Advanced Stage

The final exercise requires you to understand chords and intervals. If you don't have this level of knowledge, consider taking a theory course at your local community college or start working through *The Musical Core*.

For each of the following steps, set a timer for seven minutes. Don't spend more than five minutes on each step.

Step 1

1. Listen to a single pitched drone in your mind's' ear.
2. Add a perfect fifth drone on top of the base drone.
3. Focus on hearing this interval. Aim to make the sound of the major third as pronounced as possible until the timer goes off.
4. Repeat this process until you can complete it easily, then move on to Step 2.

Step 2

5. Mentally imagine the perfect fifth drone again.
6. Change the instrument playing the bass drone so that you are listening to two different timbres. For example, you could use a violin playing the bass drone and a trumpet playing the second drone. You're unlikely to get a perfect simulation, but do the best you can.
7. Repeat this process until you can complete it easily, then move on to Step 3.

Step 3

8. Listen to your perfect fifth drone on two different instruments.
9. Lower the pitch of the top note in the drone a half step.
10. Return to the perfect fifth drone.
11. Raise the pitch of the top note a half step.
12. Return to the perfect fifth drone.

13. While keeping the perfect fifth drone playing, attempt to hear a half step below the top drone. The goal is to hear your perfect fifth, diminished fifth, and root note at the same time.
14. Return to the perfect fifth drone.
15. While keeping the perfect fifth drone playing, attempt to hear a half step above the top drone. The goal is to hear your perfect fifth, augmented fifth, and root note at the same time.
16. Move on to Step 4 when you can complete this step successfully.

Step 4

17. Hold your perfect fifth drone mentally in your mind.
18. Add a third tone (an interval of your choice) below your existing drone and attempt to listen for five minutes.
19. Try to keep the two sounds at a specific interval. If you can't identify the interval you're hearing, that's okay, but you should get on those ear training exercises quickly.

Once you complete the exercise with a perfect fifth, try it with the following intervals: perfect fourth, major third, minor third, major sixth, minor sixth, major seventh, and minor seventh. Move along the sequence in the proper order by listening o the perfect fourth before you move on to the major third.

While listening to music in your head, it will not sound like the music you might hear in a concert hall. Music in your mind is hazy and less clear. Sometimes you'll be able to hear the music in extreme and realistic detail, but I find you have to be in a state that is near sleep for this to happen. The state that exists right before sleep is a good state for the initial realization of a composition, but it's not very effective for composing. This is because the moment you begin to notate your music, you'll lose the clarity of the music. If you have a good musical memory, then you can begin to overcome this limitation.

Chapter 12: Practical Voice Leading

CREATING INTERESTING CHORDS

If a composer could say what he had to say in words he would not bother trying to say it in music.

~ Gustav Mahler

Many composers know how to write music using traditional chords. It's a relatively straightforward and easy thing to do once you've learned music theory. However, I don't believe the role of a composer is to regurgitate what already exists. Instead, you need real techniques that will help you to create your chords while staying firmly rooted in practices that make sense.

This chapter concentrates on using voice leading rules to create effective chord progressions. With the right voice leading, you can make just about any composition sound good. Whether it's something that people will want to listen to will still depend on your ability to write a compelling piece. However, an understanding of voice leading will help most any composer to create chord progressions that work.

Following the Path of the Masters

For a long time, the main method of teaching composers to write music was through the study of counterpoint. Counterpoint helps composers create rounds, fugues, and compositions with multiple independent melodic lines occurring simultaneously.

Theory came along after the introduction of counterpoint. At first, theory was viewed by many as an overly academic subject with little relation on the composition of original works. Over time, theory became more entrenched in our educational system for composers. While theory is a useful way to emulate the styles of past composers quickly, a creative approach is still required to write music effectively.

Counterpoint at its essence is voice leading. The complex rules associated with counterpoint were laid down first by 16th-century composers who were aiming to find a suitable method of teaching composition to young students, which is why the species start out simple and then get increasingly complex. Today, we have much more relaxed standards, but counterpoint exercises can still help composers to create active lines.

The Basic Tenets of Voice Leading

Voice leading determines how melodic lines and chords resolve within a musical work. The basic idea behind voice leading is to resolve dissonances and create melodic lines that have a good rising and falling structure. It's important to begin reviewing these basic concepts now. In *The Craft of Music Composition,* counterpoint is discussed in more detail; however, it's enough to introduce some of the concepts now to make it easier for you to learn counterpoint when the time comes.

The Four Types of Motion

There are four basic types of motion in music. Direct motion includes the first two types of motion – parallel and similar. The other two types of motion are contrary and oblique. A composition with a good mix of all four types of motion can avoid monotony and maintain a sense of forward motion. It's important to learn how to utilize the various types of motion for the greatest effect.

Parallel Motion

In parallel motion, two or more lines move in the same direction and by the same interval class. The interval quality may change. For example, a move from a major to minor third is considered parallel motion. Parallel motion can easily become monotonous since the parallel movement destroys the sense of independence in the melodic lines. Use parallel motion sparingly.

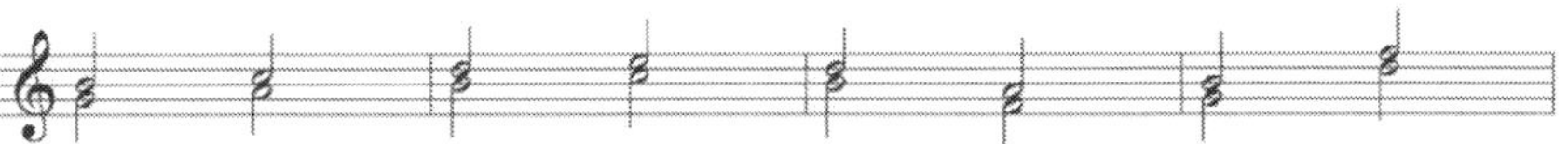

Similar Motion

In similar motion, two or more lines move in the same direction, but unlike parallel motion, they do not move with the same intervallic relationship. As with parallel motion, similar motion can become monotonous, but since the intervals do change, each melody can maintain a mild sense of independence.

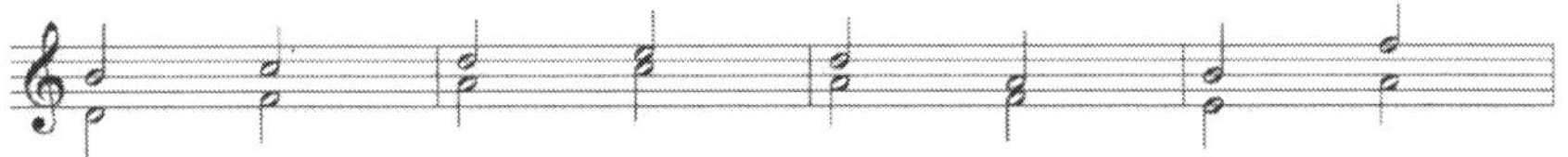

Contrary Motion

With contrary motion, two or more lines move in the opposite direction. An example would be with one line moving up while another line moves down. Contrary motion provides some of the best motion for a composition. It tends to highlight the independence of the lines, and it gives the piece a strong sense of forward motion.

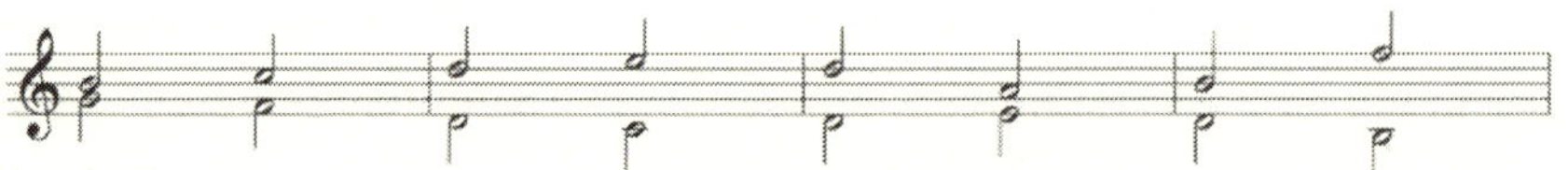

Oblique Motion

With oblique motion, one line moves while the other stays the same. Often, this results in a suspension, but since a suspension requires a preparation, suspended note and resolution, this isn't always the case. In counterpoint, the most common suspensions are 9-8, 7-6, 4-3, and 2-3 which refers to the intervals above the bass note. A ninth resolves to a consonant octave, a seventh resolves to a consonant sixth, a fourth resolves to a consonant third. In the case of 2-3, these intervals occur with a bass suspension.

Musicians debated whether the fourth was a consonant or dissonant interval during the sixteenth century. The concept of the dissonant fourth is discussed in more detail in later volumes. In the example below, the type of suspension is indicated using numbers. These numbers indicate the voice leading. Oblique motion doesn't have to utilize these specific resolutions, and it occurs anytime one voice stays the same and the other moves.

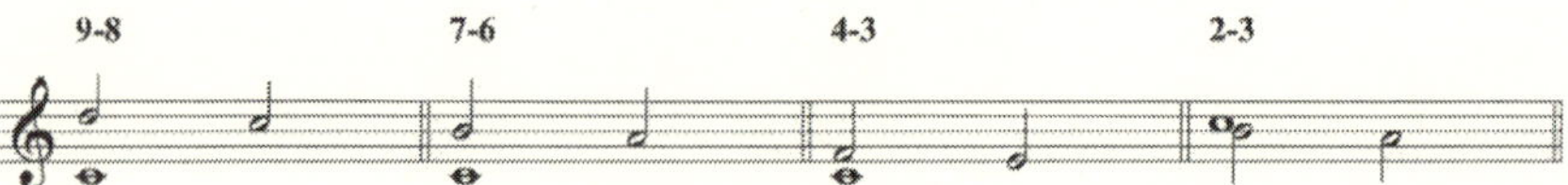

Using Voice Leading

The one motion you should avoid using is parallel motion. As noted earlier, parallel motion tends to reduce the independence of the lines. When using parallel motion, both lines tend to sound and act more like a single line. Moving in and out of parallel motion requires some artfulness. When switching from parallel motion to another type of motion, it tends to sound like an instrument was added. When you enter parallel motion, it sounds like an instrument has dropped out. In contrast, if you switch between contrary and oblique motion, the ear will always hear more than one melody.

When you use direct motion (parallel and similar motion), you risk creating musical lines with inconsistent textures. This exercise aims to teach you the value of using effective voice leading principles to fix your compositions. You can make virtually any composition sound better by avoiding direct motion.

Preparatory Exercise

Write a new composition or take one of your older pieces and review the structure for any instances of direct motion. Print your score and use a highlighter to point out any cases where both lines move simultaneously in the same direction.

Identify and then change all the instances of parallel motion so you're using either oblique or contrary motion only. Listen to your work again to demonstrate how avoiding parallel motion improves the work.

Composition Exercise

1. **Compose a Melody:** Each morning this month, compose a new melody. Make it relatively short and don't write more than 12 measures. Don't worry too much about how good the melody is; the goal is just to get you into the habit of composing daily.

2. **Create a Countermelody:** After writing the melody, write another melody to create harmony with your original melody. Write one that uses direct motion against the original melody, one that uses oblique motion against the original melody, and one that uses contrary motion in relation to the original melody.

   Both melodies should be playable at the same time. Listen to each example, and then put them away in a book or a folder on your computer. Don't think about the melodies again, and if you ever find yourself in need of inspiration, you can access these melodies to see if anything stokes the coals of inspiration.

Two things will occur if you complete this exercise every day:

1. You will start to compose more quickly.
2. You will learn the importance of paying attention to the motion used in your melodies.

Some of these melodies may never leave you, and you will find yourself playing through them in your mind at random moments throughout the year. If this happens, go back to these melodies and consider writing a piece based on them. These themes are calling to you, and they are begging to be composed. I've found that it's the melodies you can't shake that are the ones you should go back to and work out. There is one particular piece I wrote over a decade ago that still haunts me. It's a finished work, but the melody won't leave. I suppose eventually, I must revisit it.

Chapter 13: Creating Original Chords

Traditional counterpoint can aide you in the creation of original chords. Let's say you want to create a composition with chords that accompany your melody that make sense logically, but you want some new chords that aren't based on pre-existing harmonies. Voice leading can help you create progressions that make sense, even if you don't yet have a solid understanding of how to create traditional chord progressions.

As a composer, the point isn't to learn how to compose music using traditional chord progressions. The point is to learn what exists so that you know when you're creating something new. Creating new chords and progressions can prove difficult if you don't have an extensive background in music theory. Without a background in music theory, you won't know for certain if another composer has already stumbled upon your chord. However, as long as you are studying music theory, a lack of knowledge doesn't have to limit your creative spirit and sense of experimentation.

There are a few ways to create chords that work with your melody, and traditional counterpoint is one of the means to do this. Counterpoint is a complex subject that would typically take you several months to learn. However, using the technique in this lesson, you'll be able to quickly learn a practical technique that will help you to compose more effectively.

Bach used to compose a fugue every day before breakfast. They weren't always great, but the reason he could do this is that he understood counterpoint. After this lesson is complete, you will have taken the first step toward understanding counterpoint. We will not worry about the rules of traditional counterpoint. Instead, we will concentrate on learning how to create multiple independent lines that work with each other to create harmony.

Beginning Exercise

First off, you must create a theme. For this exercise, create a theme that uses primarily stepwise motion. If you need to leap (interval of a fourth or larger), then resolve that leap by moving in the opposite direction. So, if you leap from C4 to A4, you should follow that by moving down by step to G3. Skips (interval of a third) can be treated differently. A skip doesn't have to resolve in the opposite direction but avoid using more than two skips in a row.

As you complete your composition exercises, you have two rules to follow:

1. Use stepwise motion primarily. For example, moving from C4 to D4 is a step. Moving from C4 down to B3 is also a step.
2. Resolve leaps in the opposite direction of the original leap and avoid more than two skips in a row. Additionally, if you do leap, the contrary resolution should be a smaller interval than the initial leap. So, if you leap a perfect fifth, you should resolve down by a leap of a fourth or smaller.

If you're a beginning composer, then just worry about creating melodies this month. Beethoven used to work out his themes extensively, and he was known for keeping a sketchbook for his ideas. Marry your ideas and write at least two revisions of each melody. Editing is how you improve and get better as a composer.

Intermediate Exercise

Composers who want to take the next step should concentrate on creating counterpoints to their melodies. If you don't yet understand counterpoint, you can follow these basic rules to create a counterpoint to a melody that follows the "spirit" of counterpoint. The rules are broken down into instructions for creating a two-part counterpoint with two melodies.

Melody 1 (Treble)

1. Start and end on the first scale degree, so the melody should begin and end on the same note on a strong beat.
2. For the second to last pitch, include the pitch that occurs on the seventh scale and resolve this by step to the pitch you created in the first step. The penultimate pitch should occur on a strong beat. (In C, the seventh scale degree is B.)
3. Ideally, the penultimate pitch should be on a weak beat and the final pitch should fall on a strong beat.
4. Write a melody that uses primarily stepwise motion and skips.

Melody 2 (Bass)

1. Create a staff in the treble or bass clef.
2. Use the third scale degree for your beginning and ending pitches. (In C, the third scale degree is E). Make sure you place the third scale degree below Melody 1.
3. Use the second scale degree for your penultimate pitch and pair it with the seventh scale degree from Melody 1.
4. Fill in the remaining pitches using stepwise motion, and use only thirds, fourths, and sixths for the intervals between your first and second melody.

5. The perfect fifth and perfect octave may be used, but only if you don't approach the fifth or octave using direct motion (parallel or similar motion).

General Guidelines to Follow

1. Avoid multiple skips in the composition. Generally, try to resolve a skip in the opposite direction, but this is not required.
2. Check the intervals between both parts. Use only consonant intervals, but carefully use the fifth and octave since direct motion into a perfect consonance should be avoided.
3. Make sure your new melody doesn't have an interval of a second or seventh between the two melodies.
4. **Note:** an interval of a seventh and the seventh scale degree are not the same thing.

Advanced Exercise

For the advanced exercise, it's time to add a third melody to your composition. This line is the bass line. The bass line should also begin and end on the first pitch of the melody. However, when you write the bass line, you're also allowed more freedom to skip around.

Once you have completed a melody and a counterpoint to the melody, you can continue to this advanced exercise. Don't move on to this exercise unless you are comfortable with the first two exercises.

1. Create a third staff in the bass clef.
2. The first and last pitch should use the first scale degree.
3. Write the generic interval quality between the staves of Melody 1 and Melody 2. If you created Melody 1 and 2 correctly, you should write the number "3".
4. Fill in the remaining chord members that haven't yet been used. You can use them in any octave but follow the guidelines below.

   For example:
   - If the counterpoint uses a pitch that is a third above the melody, you may use the pitches that correspond to a fifth or sixth above the Melody 2 note.
   - If the counterpoint uses a pitch that is a sixth above the melody, you may use the pitches that correspond to a third or fourth above the Melody 2 note.
   - If the counterpoint uses a pitch that is a fifth or octave above the melody, you may use the pitch that corresponds to a third above the Melody 2 note. (Only if you used fifths)

Note the example that indicates how to construct your bassline. The intervals are indicated between the first and second melody. Between the second and third melody, the intervals are inverted. So, the first measure of Melody 1 includes an E and a sixth above the note in Melody 1 was used to create the C in Melody 3.

All Levels: Editing the Composition

Once the composition is complete, go through the piece and change the melody based on your personal preferences. Try making some of the notes a half-step higher or lower if something doesn't sound right. Use the existing melodies as a framework for a more involved composition.

Practice these exercises daily for a month. Always listen to the final compositions. You can play your pieces on an instrument or use a sequencer or notation program to play them back. As you improve, you'll leave the training wheels that this lesson provides in the past. Then, you'll be creating music that is truly original. Most importantly, once you learn how to treat the fifth and octave and improve your knowledge of theory, you'll be able to create increasingly complex musical works.

Chapter 14: Motives

A symphony must be like the world. It must contain everything.

It's not just conquering a summit previously unknown, but of tracing, step by step, a new pathway to it.

~ Gustav Mahler

The Building Blocks of Music

What Are Your Motives?

Motives are the building block of a composition. If you've ever heard the expression that genius begins at the fifth bar, it's because the fifth bar is traditionally where the second phrase begins. What the composer does from there is what makes the piece succeed or fail. Any decent composer can come up with a fun motive, but it's the brilliant composer that can modify and manipulate that motive into something entirely new and interesting.

Bach stated that he could take any four notes and create a composition based on those notes. Carefully, he pointed out that the piece might not be a masterpiece, but it would be effective, fully functioning and well-crafted. Bach could write effective compositions because he had a solid understanding of his craft, and he knew how to manipulate any musical material to meet his needs. In fact, Bach did just that. He wrote a piece using the letters of his name.

In German musical nomenclature, the note B♭ is a B, and the note B is an H. This is why he could create the BACH motive used in his unfinished fugue within his Art of Fugue, BWV 1080, Fuga a 3 Soggetti ("Contrapunctus XIV") collection. The four notes, B-A-C-

B♭, are an example of a motive. Bach uses it throughout the piece in creative ways, and it's one of the smallest, complete musical ideas in the composition. It can be seen beginning in measure 192 of the actual score or the second, third, and fourth measure in the illustration.

Bach had to write the notes in a specific order, so by choosing this motive, many of his choices were taken from him. Because of this, part of the compositional process was completed for him. The next step was to choose the note values and rhythm for the fugue. Once that was done, it was a matter of using it in a recognizable way.

Composition Exercise

For the next month, you will write a motive per day. I don't expect you to write a full-fledged fugue, but you should aim to create memorable motives like Bach's BACH motive. The goal of this exercise is to help you build your composition technique through a regular exercise easy to complete. Over time, you may find you want to start combining motives to create melodies. The important thing is to get in the habit of creating something every day.

Guidelines for Creating Motives:

1. Make the motives short. Keep each motive to about three to six notes.
2. Aim to create a memorable motive by using unique rhythms or pitch combinations.
3. Write the motive down by hand. It's not enough to think up a motive, you must write it down.
4. Play the motive back in your mind without the use of an external device.
5. Use rhythm, intervals, and harmony to create your motive.

Motives should be short and only four to five notes. If a motive ends up becoming too long, it's hard for the audience to follow. Think of music in your life that is memorable. Many of them use short and easy to recognize motives. A motive is not a melody, but a short, distinct idea that recurs throughout the piece.

Writing the motive down helps to make it real for you. When you sit down to notate your motives, you see the realization of that motive in a tangible form. It also helps to connect the musical ideas in your mind to music notation, which can then be edited and distributed for others to hear. Similarly, playing the motive back without an external device helps you to develop your internal ability to hear the music. Motives can manifest as rhythm, a set of defined intervals, or harmony.

Everybody should be able to complete all the following exercises. If you have the time, consider writing one motive for each level every day. Writing out a few motives shouldn't take you over five to ten minutes. The goal is to create a simple, daily routine you can always work on, regardless of how strapped you are for time.

Beginning Exercise

Create a memorable rhythm using the following guidelines. Breaking these guidelines is perfectly alright if a better way presents itself.

1. Write a simple three- to six-note rhythm.
2. Think carefully about what makes your rhythm unique.
3. Put intention behind the creation of your rhythm and consider whether your rhythm evokes a feeling or emotion.
4. If it's not interesting, edit it until it is.

Intermediate Exercise

Motives may use specific intervals. For example, a major sixth followed by a minor third could act as a two-note motive. Write a series of non-rhythm defined intervals. The rhythm shouldn't matter here. What's important is that you are creating a series of intervals that convey a mood or tone. If you've read *The Elements of Music Composition,* you already know all of the ways that motives can be created.

Create a motive using the following intervals as the basis for the motivic idea: perfect fifth, perfect fourth, major third, minor third, major sixth, minor sixth, major seventh, and minor seventh.

Advanced Exercise

Harmony uses certain chords in a similar progression to create a harmonic motive. For example, a major chord on C, followed by a minor chord on D# is a very memorable succession of harmonic chords. Used repeatedly, this could turn into a motive.

Create a memorable two or three chord motivic progression. Like the other motives, it should convey a particular mood or emotion. If it doesn't make you feel anything, then keep trying until you can create a more exciting motive. You don't need to try harder, but you need to keep composing and working at least a few times a week. Eventually, you will develop the ability you crave. Gustav Mahler famously uses a major-minor chord progression prominently in his symphonies that indicates important moments throughout the work.

Enhancing Your Motives

While we've briefly covered most of the topics in this section in *The Elements of Music Composition* text; I will review important points so you can create even more effective musical works. However, it's important to read through the Elements text for a complete understanding of motivic development.

1. **Repetition:** Repetition is unnatural and should be avoided.
2. **Rhythm:** Several methods of creating rhythm are possible that go beyond the standard uses.

3. **Motives:** The building blocks of music, learn how to incorporate motives into a composition.
4. **Rhythmic Modifications:** A discussion of several simple methods to create interesting and dynamic rhythms.

Repetition

"Don't do something a copyist could do!" Arnold Schoenberg told this to his students when encouraging them to avoid repetition. He is not the only composer who felt this way. Gustav Mahler also felt that "every repetition is a lie."

Composers have followed this general advice for centuries. Understanding what this means is essential to your technique as a composer. Repetition is often an easy way to add fluff to a composition (not desirable), and it rarely serves a meaningful purpose. However, it can be used to good effect in certain types of compositions. Philip Glass is well known for his minimalism techniques that use repetition in intelligent ways.

Sometimes repetition is useful when a composer is trying to create a particular effect. However, these moments are typically rare, and this technique must be used in a way that doesn't create an overly predictable musical line.

Rhythm

Rhythm is an important aspect of a composition. It helps to drive the music forward, and it can create highly effective and interesting musical lines. Writing rhythmically complex music is uncomfortable for many composers, but it's important to think about the many ways you can develop rhythm in your own compositions.

1. Rhythm makes a melody flow, making the rhythm as crucial to the music as the notes themselves.
2. An ability to write rhythmically complex lines allows for smooth flowing and sophisticated melodic lines.
3. Fixing poor rhythmic usage usually isn't too difficult. Pointing out the issue is all that is required for most composers.

It's possible to change a simple melody just by making small rhythmic changes. This is an excellent way to improve your composition and get more mileage out of your melodies.

Motives

Motives are the smallest complete musical ideas in a composition. Motives are usually combined to make melodies and they help to create change in a composition.

- A motive could be repeated at different pitch levels, a technique known as a sequence.
- Motives could progress in retrograde from the end (last note) to the beginning (first note).

There are numerous ways that a composer can manipulate a motive. Use a combination of techniques to get a more interesting and less predictable line. You could reorder the arrangement of pitches, change the note values, or create gestures that mimic the movement of the original motive. All of these things can help create variety and provide new methods of developing your composition.

While the manner in which you modify a motive generally has a specific name, I refer to any instance where the motive uses a similar movement as a gesture. It helps to think about the idea of motivic creation less literally, so you don't fall into the trap of over analyzing every single note in your work. Be careful with "gestures" as they must relate to the main idea in some substantial way. You can use the same rhythm, general melodic shape, or use one or use easily identifiable intervals that relate to the original melody.

While it's helpful to think generically about musical ideas when composing, it's also important to know the names for the techniques you use in a composition for the editing process. There are specific terms used to describe the different gestures. The following are a few of the most common ones:

1. **Augmentation**: Notes values are increased proportionally across the motive. For example, a quarter note becomes a half note. A half note becomes a whole note.
2. **Diminution**: Note values are decreased proportionally in value.
3. **Elision**: Notes are removed from the original motive.
4. **Fragmentation**: The motive is broken up into even smaller parts.
5. **Interpolation**: New tones are added to the motive.
6. **Isomelos**: The same notes are used, but the rhythm is changed.
7. **Interval Expansion or Contraction**: Smaller intervals are used with the same basic shape or larger intervals are used with the same basic contour.
8. **Octave Displacement**: Notes of the motive are moved to a different octave to create a disjointed line. This is great for creating a sense of panic.
9. **Ornamentation**: Trills and other ornaments are added to the motive.

10. **Permutation**: The order of the pitches is changed.
11. **Retrograde**: The motive is played backwards.
12. **Shaping**: The motive is shaped using a combination of dynamics and time. For example, a swell that lasts three seconds, on any pitch, and ends in an accent will be easily recognizable.
13. **Subcomplex**: Non-consecutive notes are removed and played over a short span of time to create a quick jolt of activity.

This list is a set of basic modifications that may work in a composition provided you think carefully about how the changes add to the work. Think about ways to incorporate these basic types of modifications in your work when it is workable. It is not a good idea to do this for the sole purpose of changing your motives without a musical purpose; however, thinking about the shape of the melody and possible improvements is an essential part of composing.

The next step involves create flowing textures by filling in the composition with changing rhythmic values. Of course, you should always strive to incorporate your motives in any modification that you make to your music.

Using your basic motive, it is possible to change the rhythm to create unconventional rhythms. By constantly stretching yourself to think "outside the box," you find that writing elegant musical lines gets easier.

Incorporate some of these modifications in your own compositions so it becomes easier to create music using non-standard rhythms. Composers should be able to notate anything they can conceive and imagine. If you have trouble writing rhythms outside of sixteenth and eighth notes, then you are missing a valuable compositional skill. Composers train to have the ability to write anything they can imagine. Even if we do not write complex rhythms in our published works, composers should still continually work to improve their rhythmic palette.

Chapter 15: The Restricted Note Composition

If you think you're boring your audience, go slower not faster.

~ Gustav Mahler

If you remember the story of Bach, you'll know he continually challenged himself to compose works based on restrictions. When you restrict what you're permitted to do, you end up with a composition that is more creative. By eliminating many of your choices, you have fewer decisions to make. This makes it possible to concentrate on the composition without having to worry about a world of limitless possibilities. Even with restrictions, you still have a vast array of choices. This exercise is designed for the advanced composer who wants to refine their skill through the completion of a composition every week.

The Restricted Note Composition is an assignment that makes it easy to find out your weaknesses as a composer. When your choices are limited, you'll be able to more clearly see where your problem areas fall and come up with techniques to improve your overall technique.

Regardless of your preference or style, the fundamental issues that affect your music will be present in most any composition you create. By limiting what you can do, you eliminate many problems that could be more complicated to correct in a larger work by eliminating the fluff of a composition and concentrating solely on your technique.

This exercise is based on the form of the Bartok String Quartets, and it is also very similar to an introductory assignment from Daniel Asia at The University of Arizona. I've made my own modifications to make it specific to the goals I wish to achieve in this lesson. There is no beginning, intermediate, and advanced technique for this chapter. You'll challenge yourself at whatever level are at by completing this exercise.

Composition Exercise

Write a piece that is approximately 5 minutes in duration (1 minute per movement) written for a solo instrument. If you've made it this far, you are now ready to compose. Create a composition that is at your level and use the following rules to limit your options and challenge your creativity.

The Note Restrictions

This composition uses note restrictions to challenge your creativity and see how well you can write when limited. Each composition has different restrictions listed at the end of this lesson. By limiting the pitches employed, more effort can be applied towards the other elements of the composition such as rhythm and articulations.

In the first movement you may pick six notes to use in your composition. These could be any notes. For illustrative purposes, we will use the notes C, C#, D#, F, G, and A. These pitches may be replicated at any octave freely. The important thing is that you are very careful to use only six notes (and their octave equivalents). You may also duplicate these notes as much as you like. Please don't take this literally and write a piece with just six notes from beginning to end! That would be a short composition.

Note Values

Each movement has different limitations on note values. Abide by these restrictions to push yourself to write a creative work.

In the first movement you should use only whole notes, half notes, and quarter notes, and their equivalent rests. You may tie notes to make longer note values, such as a half note tied to a quarter note to make a dotted half note, but only do this in a logical manner. This means you should only use a tie across a bar line. See how creative you can get when your options are limited.

It is perfectly okay to tie notes across the bar line, change the time signature, change metronome markings, and use other performance indications to change the duration of the notes. In fact, this is highly encouraged.

Performance Markings

If you write a piece that consists only of notes and does not have any dynamic markings, you have failed to write a complete work. The articulations and performance markings are as important as the notes being used. Use accents and mood indicators (i.e. *Allegro, Misterioso,* etc) to give the performer the information they need to play the piece well.

Dynamics and performance indicators are one of the most often neglected aspects of a musical creation. Students often write the notes but fail to show how they would like it performed. If this describes you, then get out of the habit of doing this now. Learn to think of all the elements of a composition at once and see them as inseparable from each other.

I'm not going into detail on the elements of a musical work and how they combine since that was the purpose of *The Elements of Music Composition*.

Nobody has ever played your music before; make sure you give them enough information to do it correctly.

Restricted Note Composition Rules

Movement 1

- **Dynamics:** Keep the dynamic level between *p - mp.*
- **Tempo:** The tempo should be slow, *Adagio* to *Andante* at the fastest.
- **Mood:** Melancholy or contemplative.
- **Note Values:** Half, whole, and quarter notes, and the equivalent rests.
- **Pitches:** Use 6 pitches only

Movement 2

- **Dynamics:** Keep the dynamic level between a *mp – mf.*
- **Tempo:** The tempo should be moderate, *Andante* to *Moderato* at the fastest.
- **Mood:** Keep the mood calm and satisfied with a sense of purposeful motion.
- **Note Values:** Half, whole, quarter notes, eighth notes, and the equivalent rests.
- **Pitches:** Reuse 3 pitches from the first Movement and choose 2 new pitches that have not been used yet.

Movement 3

- **Dynamics:** Keep the dynamic level between a *p – ff.*
- **Tempo:** The tempo should be fast, at least *Moderato* and as fast as *Presto*. This movement is the center of the composition, so try to make it the high point of the composition.
- **Mood:** Agitated, hurried, and frantic. This movement should show off your skill.
- **Note Values:** No Limitations.
- **Pitches:** Use any pitches you wish.

Movement 4

- **Dynamics:** Keep the dynamic level between a *mp – mf.*
- **Tempo:** The tempo should be moderate, *Andante* to *Moderato* at the fastest.
- **Mood:** Keep the mood calm and similar to the mood of Movement 2.
- **Note Values:** Half, whole, quarter notes, eighth notes, and the equivalent rests.
- **Pitches:** Use a pitch that was not used in either the first or second movement, which means you have 4 pitches to choose for your composition. Add this to the initial six notes from the first movement. This gives you seven pitches for the movement.

Movement 5

- **Dynamics:** Keep the dynamic level between a *p and mp.*
- **Tempo:** The tempo should be slow, *Adagio* to *Andante* at the fastest.
- **Mood:** Melancholy or contemplative. Make the mood similar to Movement 1.
- **Note Values:** Half, whole, and quarter notes, and the equivalent rests.
- **Pitches:** This movement will also have seven pitches. Use the 6 pitches that were not used in the 1st movement and 1 pitch of your choice that was used in the 1st movement.

Chapter 16: The Orchestra

One kind of artist is always striving to annihilate the past, to make the world anew in each new work, and so to triumph over the dead weight of routine. I am the other kind. I am the kind who only sees his way forward by standing on the shoulders of those who have cleared the path ahead.

~ *Steven Stucky*

Steven Stucky, a Pulitzer Prize-winning Composer, passed away from an aggressive form of brain cancer on February 14, 2016. He was diagnosed in November 2015. Cancer may have taken a great composer from us, but his legacy of music lives on in the students, orchestras, and lives he touched.

He's one of those composers who broke into the industry late. He was 38 years old before he got his first real composition job. He died when he was only 66. Toward the end of his life, he started producing some of his greatest works. His music has put him into the history books as a leading composer of the twentieth and twenty-first centuries, and he arguably single-handedly saved the L.A. Philharmonic Orchestra with his unique and novel compositions.

Stucky liked to focus on the use of color to create compelling musical works in a process you can think of as "coloring" a composition. The notes you use in a composition are important, but what's even more important is that you write a piece that has a dynamic range of colors also known as timbres.

The timbres in a composition can help to add something new to a section that might otherwise be a direct repeat. It contributes to keeping your music interesting, and it can also provide an excellent way of adding a darker or lighter intonation to a melody.

I'll be discussing some of the ways you can "color" a composition by combining instruments to create new timbres. But, the goal for this chapter is to simple start thinking about color in music and to get used to hearing different instrument sounds.

Instrument Combinations

An orchestra has an array of instruments you can combine in interesting ways. There are many courses on orchestration available, so rather than focusing on how to write for the orchestra, I will concentrate on a few guidelines you can use to create colorful timbres in your composition.

Traditional Combinations

The safest combinations occur when you mix similar instruments together.

- Woodwinds work well with woodwinds.
- Brass work well with brass.
- Strings work well with strings.

The preceding combinations are apparent. If you want to get a little more complicated, then some additional combinations result in more complex timbres.

- Woodwinds and strings mix well, in most situations.
- Strings mix well with percussion instruments like the vibraphone, xylophone, and piano.

- Brass instruments nearly always stand out and don't take on the sound of other instrument families well, but there are exceptions, which I will discuss in a moment.
- The less obvious combinations occur when you mix entirely different instruments with each other.
- The euphonium, which could be thought of as a smaller tuba, mixes well with the bassoon. This instrument combination gives off a sound similar to a dark cello. The euphonium-cello mix is a good combination when you want a string sound in a Wind Symphony setting.
- Double-reeds and higher strings mix well, but the double-reed instrument will have a slightly stronger presence.
- The flute when played in the bottom octave creates a dark and murky sound when mixed with the bassoon.

Non-Traditional Combinations

Being able to experiment with new combinations of instruments is important. Experimentation and trial is how you build your sense for what works.

You can use samplers, but a sampler will play your music perfectly. Sampled sounds won't sound like a real performance will sound, and it will lack overtones. Electronic compositions don't account for a performer's need to breathe, take rest, and play complex rhythms with nuance.

Since most of us don't have an orchestra handy, one way to make up for this is by using a sampler to combine sounds. Stack the sound of a clarinet and an oboe in your sampler and see how it sounds playing the same pitch. Using a sampler can give you a general sense of how a clarinet-oboe doubling would sound -- it's wonderful.

This is also why it's so important to listen to new music while reading the score. Even if you don't understand music theory, if you follow along with the score and recording, you can learn about real-life instrument combinations and use these sounds in your compositions.

Listening and following along with a score is one of the best ways to learn about new musical sounds. IMSLP.org has a broad range of scores and recordings for listening.

Find one of your favorite pieces and listen. Aim to listen to at least one new piece a week with a score, and you'll be well on your way to uncovering your "coloring" genius.

Some General Orchestration Guidelines

While you should aim to take a complete composition course, some general guidelines will help you to improve your compositions quickly.

Voicing Considerations

- Keep at least an interval of a fifth between the lowest two voices in your composition. A fourth is acceptable, but if the piece is low, it will sound muddy. This rule is less important for higher pitched instruments in the upper end of the range. If you write more dissonant music, a tritone also works or any interval that has a slightly transparent, consonant sound, such as the minor sixth.
- When doubling instruments, if you want the instruments to combine their respective timbres to form a new one, you'll want to put both instruments in the same register. Doubling in the same register could be difficult with instruments that have a

high discrepancy in pitch register to begin with, such as a tuba and flute.

- If you want the most pleasing sounds, aim to write for each instrument in the middle of their register.
- The highest ranges are piercing.
- The middle ranges are softer and more relaxed.
- Solo ranges exist in the mid to high ranges.
- The lowest ranges sound muddier and are suitable for less-defined music.
- Carefully balance your instruments. If you have one trumpet to one flute, the trumpet will completely dominate the line. However, one flute with a trumpet can also add softness to a trumpet solo. Consider your goals and adjust the balance of instruments to fit your goals. Learning the most common combinations is where an orchestration manual is essential to get the most effective balance.

Composition Exercises

For the next few weeks, pick a score and work through the following three exercises. These exercises are arduous, but they will drastically improve your ability to create compelling music compositions. You'll also gain a more intimate knowledge of composition. The Technique Builder is not intended to teach particular concepts, but to prime your ear and thought process to complete more intense compositional work. Later volumes deal with the nuts and bolts of composition, but you must first develop your foundation.

Beginning Exercise

Get an orchestral score and listen along with the composition. At this stage, just attempt to follow along in the score while the music plays. Listen to the piece as many times as needed until you can easily follow along. Pick one instrument group to focus on and listen for the timbre of your selected group as the composition progresses. Try to focus so intently that you begin to tune out the other instrument groups.

Intermediate Exercise

Pick a piano score of a piece you love. A classical piece is a good place to start. You can find a score in the IMSLP. Yes, this is happening again. This first exercise will likely take you several hours or days. It's difficult, but it will help you connect with the notes and the music more than even several years of composing.

1. Copy the piece by hand. Copying a score by hand is time-consuming, painful, and it will be frustrating, but it will drastically improve your abilities as a composer. You'll need staff paper to accomplish this task. Take plenty of breaks and don't strain your hand as you build up strength.
2. Listen to the piece on a loop as you notate it by hand. Pay special attention to the way different instruments sound. Note the instrument combinations used by the composer.

Advanced Exercise

In this stage, you'll be attempting to develop your inner ear using music you already know well. The goal is to hear all the instruments from the compositions you've studied in the first two exercises in your mind's ear.

1. Start with a piano piece. Read the score without the music and attempt to visualize the piece playing in your mind. Hearing the music internally in your mind may take a few attempts. Go back and listen to the recording as many times as it takes until you can hear the piece.
2. Complete the same process with a small ensemble piece, such as a string quartet or woodwind quintet. Listen for the individual instruments and try to separate the different parts. This will be more challenging with a string quartet than a woodwind quintet or ensemble with differing instrument groups.
3. Listen to an orchestral work. Try to "hear" the piece in as much detail as possible. If you have trouble, listen to the piece with the score each night before you sleep. When you wake, attempt to "hear" the piece using the score only again.

Listening before you fall asleep is important. Since it will be the last thing you had listened to before you fell asleep, you'll be better able to absorb the material and develop your ability to hear it completely in your mind the next day.

A period of extended effort followed by a quick nap is a common technique used by many successful people. The brain has a tendency to concentrate on the last thing you were thinking about while awake. While you sleep, you'll find that problems are often solved for you, and you'll develop technique you didn't know you had.

Chapter 17: Compositional Style

To hell with all these theories, if they always serve only to block the evolution of art and if their positive achievement consists in nothing more than helping those who will compose badly anyway to learn it quickly.

~ Arnold Schoenberg

If you listen to any two composers who lived at about the same time, you'll notice that each composer has a unique style and voice. How does this happen? How is it that a writer who uses the same rhythms and scales to compose is able to create a piece that sounds uniquely their own? When you listen to Beethoven, you can identify it's a piece by Beethoven. Similarly, when you listen to Mozart, you'll immediately be struck by how Mozart-y the composition sounds. Master composers have a unique and personal compositional style that emanates an individual, stylistic voice.

Many composers will model their compositions on a style of music they like, such as a theme song from a movie, or a composer they idolize. And while imitation may be the greatest form of flattery, what is the purpose of a composer who imitates? Why would a listener or music enthusiast want to listen to an unoriginal composition from a copycat when they could listen to source material instead?

Some may argue that when a composer imitates another composer's style, they are attempting to improve upon it. There is some merit to this. If this is the goal of the imitator, it's not the worst goal a composer could have. However, if you want your compositions to reflect your ideas, experiences, and all the things that make you unique, the path of imitation will ultimately leave your compositions with a hollow quality. One purpose of writing music is to express yourself when words fall short. For many composers, personal expression is what fuels their composing habits. Don't be afraid to create your own style. If it's authentic and crafted well, people will be receptive to it.

A caveat: if you're a young composer just starting out, imitating the style of a composer whose music you enjoy can be an excellent way to learn. My objection is to the composers who attempt to make a living off another composer's personal style.

What is it about Beethoven that makes his music unique from that of Mozart, Haydn, and Handel? Is it a chord progression; the way a composer assembles a melody; the instruments used?

The following exercises will help you differentiate between these important composers and will train your ear to begin recognizing the stylistic differences in other composers' works.

Composition Exercise

Download a recording and score for one of your favorite compositions, you'll be using these scores as you complete the exercises for this chapter. I've also provided a suggestion, which can be searched for and downloaded from IMSLP.org and other sources. I have also included them in the download area for the Daily Routine and Mirror Exercises.
https://mailchi.mp/5f3eab74b0ad/uremusic

- **Beethoven:** Piano Sonata No.32, Op.111: I. Maestoso
- **Mozart:** Piano Sonata No. 8 in A Minor K. 310: I. Allegro Maestoso

Beginning Exercise

The beginner can gain quite a lot just from completing the Beginning (although strenuous) Exercise. The intermediate and advanced composer may also enjoy polishing their skills by completing the Beginning Exercise in this section, so it's highly recommended that composers of all levels start with the Beginning Exercise and, if feasible, work their way up.

This activity requires nominal skill and will help you develop your inner ear and your ability to read and compose music. While I refer to the Beethoven and Mozart piece throughout, if you chose different pieces, you can still apply the concepts listed below.

1. Listen to the Maestoso section of the Beethoven and Mozart pieces three times through without the score.
2. Listen to the Maestoso section of the Beethoven and Mozart pieces three times through with the score. The goal is to listen three times through without getting lost, so you may end up having to listen over three times. If you get lost, try to find out where you are in the music. Don't stop the music; instead do your best to find your place and catch up. When the piece ends, try listening again, and this time, aim not to lose your place by following along with the score even more diligently.
3. Write out the first page of the Mozart and Beethoven Maestoso section by hand. There are plenty of places online to print staff paper, but you should probably keep some on hand anyway since you're a composer.

Writing the music by hand may take you hours. You may become frustrated or angry as the process causes your hand to cramp up horribly as it did mine when I worked to complete this assignment in university. All I can say to that is welcome to the wonderful life of a composer!

You might think this assignment is a waste of time, and you might even curse me for assigning it to you, but take the time to finish this exercise and you will undoubtedly improve your technique. Keep in mind that composers wrote entire operas and symphonies by hand before the advent of score writing software. Copying the first page of a score is nothing compared to what the composers of the past suffered through.

Why do I need to copy everything by hand?

If you start working on this exercise, after about 30 minutes you'll begin to see what's happening. If you listen to the piece with the score, you will gain familiarity with the work. Then, once you've gone through those initial steps, you will know what the piece sounds like. Finally, when you copy the score out by hand, you're going to vaguely hear it playing back in your mind. You won't be able to help it. This is the kind of activity that will improve your ability to hear music internally, and it will also help you associate a written score with audible music. When you become proficient at this skill through repeated practice, you'll eventually be able to look at a score and hear what it sounds like in your head.

Intermediate Exercise

Did you complete the first exercise as prescribed? If not, you need to go back to the Beginning Exercise and complete it in its entirety. It's absolutely necessary that you stay the course in regard to these assignments and complete them as prescribed if you want to see real results. I'll wager that if you're writing music, you're using a notation program to assist you. Keep in mind that there is no single, great classical composer living today, or ever, who hasn't written by hand at some point in their life. If you've never written music organically, with pencil and manuscript paper, you're missing out on a valuable technique.

When I was starting out as a composer, I used to sketch my ideas by hand and then used a computer to input my music. Now, I experiment mostly in my mind's ear. I've gone through the process of writing out my musical ideas by hand in the past, and my training has been long enough that I've developed the ability to hear my compositions internally. I can judge accurately how long a piece will be based on the melody. I understand that by evaluating the motives that make up a melody, the form of a composition can be determined. This is a skill that all advanced composers should possess.

However, I now use a computer to notate my ideas because it's a timesaving issue for me. When I do use a notation program, I often won't use the built-in audio to hear my music. Most notation programs strip the natural overtones of a note, and this creates an unrealistic view of what your composition may sound like.

Even with a good sampler, a significant amount of effort needs to be employed to get a realistic sound. It's better to simply develop your ear and learn to compose without an instrument or notation program. Ultimately, taking the time to develop your inner ear helps you become a more flexible, efficient, and effective composer.

Comparing Mozart and Beethoven

Let's go to look at both the Mozart and Beethoven's scores to see if we can find out what makes Mozart sound different from Beethoven.

Look at the melody from the Mozart piece and identify five things about this theme that stand out to you as notable characteristics. Once you've come up with five things, check the answers on the next page to see if any of them are similar. You need not come up with the same answers, but they should give you an idea of what to look for in music.

Think hard, get creative, and come up with five words or short descriptions you could use to describe this melodic idea.

Wait! Go to the next page when you've written your answers.

Possible Mozart Answers

- The melody begins with a dotted-eighth to sixteenth note rhythm. It's later reinforced in the second measure. This is an example of a specific answer.
- Mozart skips down to the B and then up to the E. He holds that note before moving in stepwise motion down to the A.
- Mozart creates a "ceiling" in the composition with that E and holds it before briefly going one step higher with the F and then quickly running away.
- Mozart uses slurs to identify the different parts of the melody, and this also changes the way the pianist performs the piece.
- Mozart separates his melody by using a single line without heavy chords to weigh it down.

Now, look at the melodic idea from the Beethoven piece. Identify five terms or phrases you could use to describe this melody. Go on to the next page once you've written your answers. The answers don't matter as much as the process of coming up with five terms or phrases.

Wait! Go to the next page only when you've written your answers.

Possible Beethoven Answers

- The melody uses commanding motives with dense, deliberate, and strong attacks.
- Beethoven uses thick harmonies to create dense, powerful hammering chords.
- The dynamic range is dramatic, with Beethoven quickly going from forte to an even heavier sforzando, from a delicate piano to a ripping forte.
- Beethoven uses trills and ornaments to create a dramatic and florid composition.
- Rests are used for carefully orchestrated breaks between intervals. This helps to add dramatic effect to the composition. Here, the music is in the silence.

Advanced Exercise

Now that we've looked at a small excerpt from the Mozart and the Beethoven piece. Let's use our notes to figure out what makes the Beethoven piece sound different from the Mozart piece.

We have ten points total we can use to compare to both pieces. Now we must look at the work as a whole to determine if our generalities can be applied at large.

Let's look at my first point about Mozart:

"The melody begins with a dotted eighth to sixteenth note rhythm. Mozart later reinforces this idea in the second measure."

Does Mozart do this throughout the piece? As you'll note in the score, the answer appears to be yes, he uses a dotted eighth to sixteenth note figure throughout the piece to help tie things together. This could be a stylistic aspect of Mozart to look out for in his other works.

Does Beethoven do this as well? The answer is also yes. Beethoven uses the same type of rhythm throughout the work, which means both Mozart and Beethoven are using the same type of rhythm. But that doesn't mean the two composers are using this idea in the exact same way.

Don't get caught up in the little details here. Yes, both composers are using a rhythm that sounds very similar. However, there is one thing that makes Beethoven sound different and it goes back to one of the other observations – he's more dramatic. He uses faster note values, so that his 32nd notes sound sharp and crisp. However, both motives essentially have the same "spirit."

So, what really makes Mozart sound different from Beethoven?

- Mozart's lines are mostly single melodic lines; Beethoven uses the entire keyboard to pound out dense harmonies.
- Mozart writes with extreme clarity where each note of the melody in the work can be heard on its own; Beethoven writes in a way where the notes and melody are less important than the resounding reverberations of the chords and the density. True, a clearly defined melody with crisp and light chords is a signature aspect of most classical works, and Beethoven really was a composer who was on the verge of the romantic period. However, these differences in conjunction with the composer's own inspired compositional process are what make these pieces unique.
- Mozart writes for clarity of melody and harmony; Beethoven writes strong chords and powerful rhythms, with less emphasis on melody and more emphasis on motives.

Go through your entire list and compare each answer in the Mozart to the characteristics present in the Beethoven score. If you find similarities, search for the subtle ways that each composer makes those techniques their own.

For example: I stated in the Beethoven piece, "The melody uses commanding motives with dense, deliberate, and strong attacks." Is this true for Mozart as well? I would argue the answer is no. Mozart aims for lightness, clarity, and uniformity; Beethoven aims for strength, power, and density.

Analyze both compositions in this way, and you'll find out what makes each composer unique. Do this with any new composer you come across. Look for the special voice and stylistic things they do to make their compositions stand out as their own. By doing this, you'll develop a more refined ear and think more critically about your own compositions.

While you should strive for accuracy, it's less important that you're getting the answer right when analyzing a composition from another composer. The important thing is that you're pushing your ear to make comparisons and contrasts between the works of various composers. Going through this process will help you to develop a better ear for subtleness in music. This will only help make your compositions better.

Analyzing Music Scores

If you've completed the beginning, intermediate, and advanced portion of this lesson don't stop there. If you have time, pull up two more works by composers you aren't familiar with. Copy the first page of the score and work through these stages again. Make this exercise one of your valued tools you use to analyze, understand, and improve your understanding of music.

In the previous assignment, you may have learned that Beethoven uses commanding chords, strong accents, and clearly defined rests in his music. You also may have discovered how Mozart writes delicate lines that cater to and evoke a sense of balance and uniformity. Mozart breaks up his chords instead of playing them simultaneously, which is in dramatic contrast to Beethoven's predilection for packing chords together tightly to achieve greater density and power.

Now, let's say you want to compose a lighthearted section in your work, you know that you must thin out the texture in a Mozartian way. At this point, you could study more Mozart scores to uncover his secrets and apply the techniques to your own works. If you want a denser texture, you may dust off a Beethoven score and delve deeper into how he voices his chords for the most potent and powerful effect. Bringing your knowledge of music theory knowledge into the mix, and you'll begin to see how Beethoven uses inversions of chords for less stable sections and root position chords to restore stability.

As you develop as a composer, you will assemble a collection of ideas based on an understanding of other writers' works. Learning what makes one writer different from another makes it possible to avoid those processes in your own music. Through greater analysis and understanding, you can avoid pure imitation; you'll learn why a composer uses a particular technique, which in turn, helps you to make more intelligent choices. When you see that composers are intentional in the way they compose their music, you won't be able to help but think more intently about your own.

Once you know "the why," you can absorb the concepts used by other composers into your own technique and make it your own. This is in stark contrast to simple imitation, where you attempt to copy another composer's melodies, chords, and forms while never attaining a real understanding of the techniques they spent a lifetime refining. True composition involves thinking about the nature of music to create your own set of rules that are based on sound principles. Composing also requires you to take a step back and realize that theory is intended only as a roadmap of the music of the past. Music theory does not create, it only codifies and analyzes what already exists. As a composer, you need to think about music theory in a creative way and use it as a guidepost to understand the principles that the composers of the past employed to write their music.

Score analysis is the bedrock of composition technique. Learn from those who came before you and study their techniques. You need not be a theory whiz to look at a score and see what a composer is doing. With nothing more than the knowledge of a few note names and some basic rhythms, we were able to analyze two scores in this lesson and gain some valuable information. You can complete a basic score analysis activity with any composition you come across. Don't just listen to new music. Analyze it and try to figure out what makes it tick. While it's helpful to analyze chord progressions, the ability to complete a useful chordal analysis is a more advanced technique based on the same thinking outlined in this lesson. However, it's also important you open up a theory textbook or continue on to *The Craft of Music Composition* so that you're not reinventing the wheel and creating a new, non-standard set of terms for elements that theorists have already discovered.

Anybody can be taught to analyze a piece of music, figure out the chords used and identify a chord progression. Understanding the nuances that a writer uses to create their works and individual style is a much more valuable skill. The technique learned in this lesson can apply to any style of music. If you don't have a score, you must be a little more abstract and focused while listening to the audio recording.

I should mention that the method I discussed in this lesson is just a surface level method of analyzing a composition. A more in-depth explanation would require an intensive discussion of motives, how they are used to develop a composition, a concept known as organic music, and the principles of cohesion and comprehensibility. These are topics I discuss in *The Elements of Music Composition* text.

Chapter 18: The Phrase

I am hitting my head against the walls, but the walls are giving way.

~ Gustav Mahler

The structure for a composition provides the container you can use to help your listener make sense of your melodies, motives, and rhythm. Without structure, music meanders and lack direction or focus. Individual composers have successfully written compositions without structure in the past, but these types of forms are rare and require a matching musical style. For example, 12-tone music, while highly organized and formal, can be written without form in mind since the organization is found in the sequence of notes themselves.

Rather than throw a group of forms at you that may or may not be useful to your aims, I will discuss how you can take a melody and expand the melody. When you break it down, most forms can be analyzed as part of a two-part (binary) or three-part (ternary) system. However, since this isn't a course on musical form, we're going to focus only on breaking down the phrase into antecedent and consequent phrases.

Antecedent and Consequent Phrases

In most melodies, there is an antecedent and consequent phrase. Most times, both parts will be of approximately the same length, but it's also common for the consequent phrase to be longer than the antecedent phrase. The antecedent phrase tends to end with an inconclusive sounding cadence, which makes the piece feel like it needs to continue. The consequent phrase includes a conclusive cadence that makes the melody sound like it comes to an end.

Cadences and additional information on form are discussed in *The Craft of Music Composition* text.

Take a look at the following familiar tune that uses a series of antecedent and consequent phrases. If you play this on the piano, you may recognize this piece as 'Mary Had a Little Lamb."

I've labeled the antecedent and consequent phrases in the piece. An antecedent phrase is the first part of the phrase and the consequent phrase is meant to complete the phrase. If we had the harmony analyzed as well, there would like be a chord built on the fifth scale degree in measure 4 and a chord built on the first scale degree in measure 8. The fifth scale degree is known as the dominant and the first scale degree is the tonic. While the topic of cadences is beyond the scope of this text, more advanced musicians will recognize that measure 4 ends in a half cadence and measure 8 ends with a perfect authentic cadence.

Both phrases have a similar structure. The antecedent and consequent phrases use virtually the same musical idea, but the second part of the phrase begins to change starting in the third and fourth measure, and the seventh and eighth measure. Slight changes in a phrase showcases an example of how to use the same phrase twice with minor changes to develop the composition further.

In a composition, the phrases help to organize the entire piece. Most composers will compose their initial phrases with an understanding of how that phrase will develop over the course of a composition. An experienced composer can look at a melody and know approximately how long the piece should be, what form the composition should use, and how it's going to develop.

For example, with our initial phrase, let's say you develop this eight-measure melody, and you then decide that there is something you don't like about it. After analyzing the composition, you realize that you're mostly repeating the phrase verbatim in both sections and you would like something with a little more variety.

Since you know that the theme is broken up into two phrases, you can leave the first phrase alone and concentrate on modifying the second phrase. Notice how the rhythm stays the same and I only changed the notes. However, this will also result in an imperfect authentic cadence since the piece no longer ends with the first scale degree in the top voice.

By changing the second repetition of the phrase, I've created a less predictable composition. It's a simple change, but it makes the piece a little more sophisticated and interesting for the listener.

Now that you have your first eight measures created, you can take this a step further and think about composing the form for the piece using a variety of techniques.

Using an exact repetition is by far the easiest way to create a piece that uses binary form. However, this is something that anybody could do, and you'll probably want to change the two sections to make them more interesting.

The modified example gives you an overview of the same piece using contrasting phrases. Notice how the composition uses similar movement and pacing, but the notes changed. This phrases in each repetition are still intricately related, but the pitches have changed to make the consequent phrase more radically different.

The following exercise should be accessible to all composers. Using the information from this chapter, create a phrase with an antecedent and consequent phrase.

Try to break down your first melody into two or three motives. Then, use one motive to create the second phrase, and use the second motive to create third phrase. This will create a concept known as coherence in your composition to help make your composition more comprehensible to the listener. While coherence is an interesting concept in music composition, this text is only intended to help you develop technique. It's not intended to teach you how to be a composer, but to develop your ability to compose music.

These exercises are simple exercises that can be worked on daily. If you do this, you'll find that sometimes you get some good ideas. At other times, you might have ideas that aren't so great, but you'll always be developing your ability to work with motives.

Some composers set challenges to themselves to write a composition a day for a period of a month, quarter, or year. While you're not composing a fugue a day, this exercise will keep you creating on a daily basis and tone down that inner critic that may be keeping you from composing regularly.

Beginning Exercise

For the beginning exercise simply create melodies that can be broken down into two or three smaller motives. Aim to write one melody per day.

Intermediate Exercise

Intermediate composers should write a two-phrase piece each morning. Don't worry too much about how well the piece works. If you have a greater level of theory knowledge, then make the first phrase inconclusive with the second phrase as a conclusive cadence. For less advanced composers, end the first phrase on the fifth scale degree and the second phrase on the first scale degree. Most importantly, create two phrases that work together.

Concentrate on these important factors:

- Each melody should comprise smaller motives.
- The motives from the first phrase should appear in the second phrase of your composition.

Advanced Exercise

Advanced composers should write a three-phrase composition with two antecedent phrases and one consequent phrase in each phrase group. The antecedent phrases should be inconclusive ending on the fifth scale degree. The conclusive phrase should end on the first scale degree. Don't worry too much about how well the piece works. The goal is simply to write something every day. Remember, we're building technique. This is not a course in music composition.

Concentrate on these important factors:

- Each melody should comprise smaller motives.

- The motives should be evident in the second phrase and the third phrase of your composition.

Chapter 19: Score Preparation

All that is not perfect down to the smallest detail is doomed to perish.

~ Gustav Mahler

How to Get Rejected Immediately

In the final chapter, we'll be talking about a paramount aspect of music composition -- winning contests.

Learning how to set up a score will differ from our typical exercise-based chapters, but it's an important issue that would come up in any reputable composition seminar. I will lay out guidelines for you to follow so you don't get immediately rejected when you submit your work to a contest.

These are the tips that many composers who go to college, university, or conservatory share. They are the inside tips and bits of information that make the difference between a trained and untrained composer. Fair or not, composition contests don't always choose the most talented composer.

With so many submissions, they have to have certain rules and guidelines in place to ensure that they can consider each applicant. The practice of tossing the submissions from composers who don't follow these unspoken rules is not entirely unfair though. A composer that doesn't take enough pride in their work to do the hard editing on their composition will likely not make it as a composer. How are you supposed to compete if you don't know the rules?

If you want to get immediately rejected on your next composition contest, then ignore these rules and keep doing what you're doing. If you want your score to have a chance, and not end up immediately in the circular file, then pay attention. These rules are compulsory.

Submitting a Work Deserving of Attention

The following topics will be covered in this chapter, and while this list isn't comprehensive, it's enough to prevent your score from getting immediately dismissed.

Contest Guidelines

You need to follow the rules of the contest or publication company. Failure to do so will get your score rejected. Without guidelines, use the guidelines laid out in this booklet.

Computer Generated Scores

There is a great benefit to writing your scores out by hand. You'll feel more connected to the music, each note gets written with intention, and you'll be able to format the score exactly as you want. Having said that, don't use a handwritten score. You must use a notation program, and you need to use Finale or Sibelius to format your score.

MuseScore and other free programs have come a long way, but publishers and contests will judge you based on the program you use to submit your score.

Judges may not explicitly state this, and they will never say they rejected your score because of the notation program you used, but you better believe this happens. The judges may not even consciously know of this bias, but the thickness of the bar lines, the spacing between the staves, and even the quality of the notation will just seem amateurish.

In the beginning stages of a contest, they aren't looking at your music. They are only looking at how neat your score is. If you submit to a publisher, this is less true, and it's even less true of a university.

When you apply for a publisher or university, there may be more time to review your submission, and they may let you slide on certain score cleanliness issues, but it's better always to put your best foot forward.

The Score's Cover

The score cover is crucial. The cover needs to have the following key elements to make it easier to get an overview of your composition.

- Title of the work
- Name (or pseudonym) of composer
- Address and contact information

The title should also be printed on the spine of larger works. However, in most cases, you'll be forgiven if you don't do this. Few composers will add that little detail, but if you do, it will make your score and professionalism stand out.

The Front Page

The first page of the score needs to provide basic information:

- Full title of the work
- Approximate duration of the work
- Listing of the instrumentation

- Identification of any doublings
- Key of any transposing instruments (clarinets, horns, trumpets, saxophone, etc.)
- Percussion instruments (plus the number of percussionists that are required)
- Special instrumentation should also be noted on the front page.
- Explanation of any deviations from standard notation. For example, if you use modern notation practices, explain what each symbol means.

The Music

If the reviewer has made it this far, you're in good shape. Now is where the real work begins.

- The full name of every instrument should appear to the left of the staff system at the beginning of the score.
- Abbreviations must be used on each page that follows the main page.
- Tempo and dynamics should use English, Italian, German, or French. Choose one language and stick with it.
- Tempo indicators should always appear above the top staff and above the first violin line. With a wind symphony, it should appear again above the highest brass instrument.
- Number every measure. The measure numbers should start over with each movement. Placement of the numbers should be consistent, but they may be placed above, below, or on their own line in the grand staff.
- Rehearsal letters are not required, but they should only mark the main sections of the piece if they are used.

Score Readability

The readability of the score is a crucial part of any submission. A messy score will not get over five-seconds of consideration.

- o Use a computer. Don't submit a handwritten score unless you have no other choice. If you submit a handwritten score, you must use ink. Use velum or opaque paper if you submit a handwritten score.
- o Right-hand pages should be odd-numbered. Left-hand pages should be even numbered. Place page numbers in the top right or left corner of the page, but be consistent
- o Pay to have your score proofread. Don't do it yourself; you will not catch everything since composers often become blind to their mistakes.
- o Don't create staves with over one part on a single staff.
- o String parts should comprise a single part for each section. For instance, Violin 1, Violin 2, and Viola would all have their own staves.
- o Complex string divisions should be separated by over one staff if you write over one part on the same staff. Pro tip: Just write each part on a new staff.

Instrumental Parts

The manner in which the parts are created is the place where the professional composer is separated from the amateur.

- o Use 60 to 70 110 (100 gsm) paper. This is important to avoid see-through.
- o Use eight or ten staves per page. Don't fit over ten staves on the page.
- o Use a readable staff size of 8.5 mm. This measures from the top to the bottom of the staff. A notation program should allow you to adjust this manually. Never, ever, use anything below 7.0 mm.

- Don't number each measure. Just put measure numbers at the beginning of each line.
- Identify the measure numbers in a multi-measure rest. For example, 100-128.
- Use cues during long rests and make sure the cues are transposed to the key of the instrumental part they appear in.
- Double-check tempo and meter changes for all parts.
- Timpani should be its own separate part.
- Notate percussion instruments from highest to the lowest part.
- Aim to avoid the use of Bva and 8vb when possible. While these are acceptable in a score, it's best to avoid their use in parts.
- Write the parts for transposing instruments in the correct key.
- Don't include harp pedaling. It's best left to the performer.

Formatting Guidelines

This section will deal with the format of your parts. The suggestions here represent the standard recommendations, and they will help you to create an effective score easy to read.

- Parts should be on paper that is no less than 8 x 11 inches for the image area, but the actual paper should be at least 9.5 x 12.5 inches. Concert parts are often printed on 10 x 13-inch paper. Don't exceed 11 x 14 inches.
- The ISO A and B standard should have parts that fit within an image area of approximately 170 mm x 257 mm. The paper should be no smaller than A4. Doing so produces a 40 mm margin.
- When no instructions are provided, B4 paper is the preferred size for parts.
- Print music on both sides of the page.
- Don't use coils or bindings for parts. However, they are permissible, and often expected, for scores.

Composition Exercise

Go through your scores and edit them so they follow these minimum guidelines. Configure the default settings in your program to ensure that scores are as close to industry standards as possible. There aren't varying levels for this exercise since most any composer can follow the principles laid out in this chapter.

If you liked the text and feel it helps you to compose more effective music or understand music on a higher level, please leave a review so that others can learn from your experiences. A review is the greatest thanks I can receive!

If you're interested in additional courses, techniques, and books on music composition, please visit UreMusic.com, stay updated on Facebook (https://www.facebook.com/uremusic), or follow me on Twitter (https://twitter.com/uremusic). I would love to hear from you and discover if you found the exercises helpful.

Additional Resources

- The Musical Core Lecture Series (2018)
- The Musical Core (2018)
- The Elements of Music Composition (2019)
- Music Composition Technique Builder (2019)
- The Craft of Music Composition (2020)
- The Art of Music Composition (2024)
- UreMusic.com and UreMusic.org

The Musical Core Lecture Series

The Musical Core is a public lecture series that takes students through the basics of music theory, and it also complements the online music theory and ear training course for students who purchase access. This is a good place to start to learn about music, how it developed, and gain insight into everything from note names to chords. A more user-friendly way to access the playlist is to visit KevinUre.com and click the YouTube link.

https://www.youtube.com/playlist?list=PLoSeDrmcZDEttC4666w2b79hoWoH7S-mN

The Musical Core (2019)

If you lack basic musicianship skills, this is the course for you. It provides ear training, basic music theory and exercises to help you develop the basic skills required to hone your craft. Through a combination of online courses, you can learn the basics that are required to complete additional theory courses. Information is available at themusicalcore.com, and it is published by Kendall Hunt Publishing Company. Visit TheMusicalCore.com or KendallHunt.com for more information.

The Elements of Music Composition (2018)

Music Composition Technique Series Vol. I

The Elements of Music Composition serves as an introduction to the *Music Composition Technique Series*. It deals with the concept of coherence and comprehensibility in music so that you can begin to think about every component of a musical composition as related to the whole. This text provides the basis for a philosophy of music composition that does not demand strict theories of adherence to rules. This text details many of the concepts that I teach composers within private lessons, and it can serve as the basis for a music composition technique.

Music Composition Technique Builder (2019)

Music Composition Technique Series Vol. II

This is the next text in the series after *The Elements of Music Composition.* The technique builder includes the resources and techniques that I use with my private students to develop their inner ear and learn how to conceptualize musical works entirely in their mind. Some of the exercises have also been developed while teaching university students basic musicianship skills, so these concepts are well-planned and organized. The techniques in this book have even led in an increase in students who have developed absolute pitch, although, that is not the goal of this text by any means.

The Craft of Music Composition (2020)

Music Composition Technique Series Vol. III

For those who are interested in a more in-depth discussion of music theory topics, consider getting *The Craft of Music Composition* released in 2020. This series delves into harmony in a concise manner so that composers can integrate theory into their technique and move on with their composing lives. This text is also a great prep course for undergraduates, graduate review course, and reference for music theory instructors.

This course is based on undergraduate and graduate music theory courses I've taught, and it was developed while teaching at The University of Nevada, Las Vegas. This text is divided into two parts, Part I deals with common practice music. Part II deals with modern music theory.

The Art of Music Composition (2024)

Music Composition Technique Series Vol. IV

The art of composing deals with the process of polishing a work and the application of original ideas. Perfecting an art requires a composer who has achieved a true mastery of music and understands the theory and principles that result in effective music. This text takes the principles addressed in The Elements of Music Composition and expands on them since the composer should know have a solid education in the cornerstones of music.

UreMusic.org and UreMusic.com

Students can read about all manner of music topics at UreMusic.org. Online music composition lessons are available through UreMusic.com. If you're interested in learning about additional composition books, courses, and lessons, you can visit the website at UreMusic.com.

Recommended Textbooks

I've also included a list of textbooks that I have recommended in this book. These books do not include edition numbers or publication dates since they tend to be updated frequently.

- The Study of Orchestration. Adler, Samuel.
- Gradus ad Parnassum. Fux, Joseph.
- *Theory of Harmony*. Schoenberg, Arnold.

Manufactured by Amazon.ca
Bolton, ON

14883259R00136